The
Future
of our
Nation

The
Future
of our
Nation

ALVIN R. ERVIN

Library of Congress Control Number:		2021917390
ISBN:	Hardcover	978-1-6641-9031-3
	Softcover	978-1-6641-9030-6
	eBook	978-1-6641-9029-0

Print information available on the last page.

Rev. date: 08/17/2021

To order additional copies of this book, contact:
Xlibris
844-714-8691
www.Xlibris.com
Orders@Xlibris.com
818395

June 4, 2001

Alvin R. Ervin
Minister of the Gospel
1110 S. 24th St.
Temple, Texas 76501

Southwest Radio Church Ministries
PO Box 100
Bethany, Oklahoma 73008

Dear Dr. Hutchings,

Grace to you and peace from God, our Father, and Lord Jesus Christ.

First, I thank my God through Jesus Christ for you and all of Southwest Radio Church, that your faith will be spoken of by every person in this nation and throughout the whole world.

I pray this letter will find you in great health. I know of your past illnesses. I also know Him who is able to do *more* than we can ever ask or think. The Lord Jesus is able to breathe a new breath in you through a vision and a healing touch to cause you to desire to want to stay with us and also able to keep you with us. I believe he is lengthening your life. The prayer of faith has been prayed for you.

Dr. Hutchings, the reason that I am writing you is I heard you speak of writers and/or authors on the Southwest Radio program a couple of years back. You were discussing with another brother on the air regarding writers' ability to write and that listeners could contact you. It has taken me a while to contact you. I do pray that you can help. While I am lacking in a great ability to write, I believe my message will more than compensate: "God is a Great Deliverer, and Christ our Lord is returning soon."

I am interested in writing, and I would like to become better at it, and I do want to become an author. While studying English composition at the community college near where I lived in Irvin, Texas, I learned that there are different styles of writings. The easiest, of course, is narrative of which I use most of the time, especially regarding testimonials, which this will be, for the most part.

I know that most people would consider it kind of dinosauric writing longhand instead of a computer generating a letter, but I do not have a printer to use with my notebook computer, and also, I am enjoying writing by hand—will use the computer soon enough.

The story begins May 15, 1981, Friday night, 10:00 p.m. I was living in Temple, Texas, at the time. I had transferred my employment from Dallas while working at Texas Instruments as a manufacturing engineering planner. I picked up the phone to call the lady that I had dated for six years. It was approximately ten that night. I was merely calling to check on her and to let her know that I was thinking about her. I did not get an answer. I called back an hour later. No answer. I continued to call every hour until 1:30 or 2:00 a.m. Finally, she answered and told me that she had met someone at the church she was attending and that they were dating. Completely surprised, shocked, and hurt, I felt my world was coming apart. Please consider it was only twelve days before, on May 3, that I had gotten baptized and given my life to the Lord Jesus Christ. I knew nothing about how to call on the Lord. As a child, I dreamt of traveling and doing many other nice things in life. She was the lady in my life when many of those things happened. Now she would no longer be in my life. It was unbearable.

I began reading my Bible. Starting in Matthew's Gospel, chapter 1. Something happened when I got to chapter 21. Now all of God's Word was good up to that point, especially the Lord's Prayer in chapter 6. But when I began to read chapter 21, verse 21, it seems as isomething exploded inside. A *great* joy flooded my soul, and I felt as if I could speak to a mountain and see it move. It said, "Verily I say unto you, if ye have faith, and doubt not, ye shall not only do this which is done to the fig tree, but also if ye shall say unto this mountain, Be thou removed, and be thou cast into the sea, it shall be done." Verse 22 was equally as good: "And all things, whatsoever ye shall ask in prayer, believin, ye shall receive."

I closed the book, began to call on the Lord Jesus Christ. The more I called on Him, the more fear would come. Fear had come already, Satan telling me I would never find another lady like the one I had lost. "And why don't you kill yourself," he would say. But I continued to hold on to God's Word, reminding Him of his Word, telling Him, "You told me you would take this fear from me!" With great strength I would tell Him. I wrestled with God's Word for six full months. Just as Jacob wrestled with the angel all night, I held on to God's Word, His promise to deliver me. I was brought up in a Baptist family, with my grandmother, Celester Dotsey, and my mother, Eddie Dotsey-Jordan, teaching us "You can't kill yourself and go to heaven," so when Satan told me to kill myself, I thank God I had my parents' words to hold on to.

I continued to seek God's face, day and night, also asking Him to let me know that He was with me. The lady that I had been dating never called. She was in Dallas, and I lived here in Temple. I missed her very much and wanted to talk to her, but she never called. Then one day, for no apparent reason, she called. To say I felt great inside would be an understatement. And that would only be the beginning of great things happening in my life. When I put down the phone, a still, small voice said inside of me, "I had her to call." From that time, for the next twenty-two months or more, every day, God did something in my life to let me know He was with me and that He was answering my prayer. It culminated one Sunday there at Word of Faith World Outreach Center and Family Church, under the pastorate of Robert Tilton, in Dallas, Texas.

I was born again in Temple, Texas, at Victory Missionary Baptist Church, under the pastorate of Rev. S. E. Fowler, where later I also acknowledged my call in the ministry and licensed.

After beginning to call on the Lord with all my heart, a few months later I became active in the church. I joined the usher staff. I had heard of a friend that had given his life to the Lord but later he stopped attending church. So I purposed in my heart that I would never stop attending church, that I would forever serve God and His people. (That was twenty years ago. With God's help, by His grace I haven't stopped). After joining the ushers, I continued to have a very close walk with the Lord. I believe my pastor could see that I had a hunger for God's Word and to serve. He later appointed me director of youth ushers, of which my son Terrence joined after I joined the adults. He would follow me everywhere. When I stood up to answer the altar call, to give my life to the Lord, he stood up beside me. He was nine years old. I believe he enjoyed following because of the close relationship we had as father and son and because of the way I was training him. I did everything I could to instill in him the things of God.

After seeking God's face and serving Him for sixteen months, my transfer came through on my job that I had been trying to obtain. I moved back to Dallas. On my arrival, I saw many friends that I had not seen in a while (white, Hispanic, and black, of course, me being black). They would ask me, "When are you and Roger going to have another party?" Roger was considered my blue-eyed soul brother. He and I had had great success in bringing our friends together in ways that I would not have ever imagined. I told them, "I am not the person you knew. I do not do those things anymore."

I was very popular on my job. Plant managers with more than a thousand employees reporting to them knew of our parties, and the manager with all other managers reporting to him attended and enjoyed our parties. The first one given was at the clubhouse where I lived (my brother Hue and I), but we soon outgrew its size. We then began taking over places like the "Koo Koos Nest" at Don Carters bowling lanes. He was a professional bowler who had opened his own bowling lanes and disco, which was above the lanes.

I believe the kind of popularity (being well known and liked) that was afforded me, well, after becoming a Christian, I was no longer approached. Except by one of our friends that partied and took trips with us, Pete, who had also given his life to the Lord or had become closer to the Lord. We worked in the same department but in different areas. I had been promoted to the planning/manufacturing area where I assisted manufacturing engineers. I had not seen him very much since I moved back to Dallas, but he approached me one day and asked me to be the best man in his wedding. Please consider I am a great dreamer, and I had dreamt of guys that thought enough of me to request me being their best man. This one was white, which to me was an added honor.

So now I had begun seeing that God not only answers my prayers but also causes my dreams to come to pass. Before Peter asked me, my sister's fiancé, Tony asked me. Between the three of us, my brother Hue, who is younger than me, and my sister Reginia, who is younger than he is (thirteen years my junior), none of us at the time had any formal education. And here is Tony, a college graduate who did not know that much about me asking me to be his best man. Tony did know that I had transferred from Texas Instrument Dallas to Temple. He also knew I was the only black person occupying a desk and computer among all white managers and assistants. He also knew I was involved in the church and anyone who knew me, I believe, knew that I loved the Lord. Before Tony asked me, my brother Hue asked me to be his best man in his wedding. So within months three special people asked me to be best man in their wedding. Of all the people I partied with, I believe Pete Tracy at the time was the only one that has given his life to the Lord Jesus Christ. I pray others have come to know Him since that time.

Before serving as best man in my brother's wedding, one of my closest friends, Grady, got engaged. Our circle of best friends was Grady, Jackie, and me. Jackie was his close friend and also his cousin. So I bowed out when he approached me and said, "I do not know which one of you guys to choose," but God never forgot me, because I really did want to be Grady's best man. I believe both Grady Bolton and Jackie Crathers love the Lord Jesus Christ with all their hearts.

Dr. Hutchings, regarding dreams, I believe I owe it God and His people to share them because all of them have come true except the one I am believing that He is going to bring to pass. I have been told by some preachers that it is the gift of faith operating in me. Not only am I a dreamer, but the gift of faith is causing those dreams to come to fruition. I am sure I will have more to say about dreams as I share this story and testimony.

After moving to Dallas and joining the church that my pastor suggested I join, Rev. R. I. Samson, pastor, could see the zeal of God in me. After attending his evangelism 101 class and completing it with perfect attendance, he requested that I teach Sunday school, youth boys. I continue to serve God with great zeal.

On my way home one evening as I listened to Christian radio, I heard this Word of Faith, Spirit Fill, Tongue Talking, Faith Healing, preacher, Robert Tilton say, "Touch whatever part of your body that is sick and be healed." I was driving the second Datsun Z car that I purchased. The first one, I had completely restored. It had a telephone CB in it, and I believe I worshipped it. Thus, one early morning, approximately 1:30 to 2:30 a.m., driving home from Jackie's house, just outside the city limit of Temple, I dozed off behind the wheel. When my eyes opened my two left wheels were pulling upon the center dividing concrete structure and my car was turning over.

Please consider. I was a James Bond 007 fan when I was in the world, and I saw him drive down an alley too narrow to put his car in. I saw him put the auto on two wheels and drive down that narrow passage. I dreamt of driving a car like that on two wheels. Please know it is not all that is cracked up to be. I could feel the entire weight of that car in the steering wheel. The automobile did turn over. I got trapped in the car. I saw sparks flying while sliding down I-35 upside down. I was afraid because I was trapped. Eventually kicking the door open, I got out.

This was one of the circumstances the led me to the Lord. Two weeks before that, Grady and I was southbound on I-35 going to Austin to party. We were in his Corvette going 115 miles per hour when the car in front of us changed to our lane. To miss hitting that car, we had to change lanes. When we did, our car went into a spin. At one hundred plus miles per hour we continued to spin down I-35. That incident also helped lead me to the Lord, but that's another story.

The Datsun Z car that I had been driving was my dream car. When I totaled it out, I really missed it. So my next automobile was another Datsun Z car. This one was even nicer. It was a 280Z. The first was a 240Z. The stereo in this car was the best-sounding stereo I had ever heard in an automobile, a great mixture of treble and bass. The treble was perfect, and I have not heard one that picks up the brass section as well. It was a Jensen. It had a short in the wiring, and it was very frustrating.

When I heard that preacher say "Touch whatever part of your body that is sick and be healed," I laid my hand on that radio and the short in the system went away and never returned. A few months later, in February 1983, I moved my membership to Word of Faith so that I could hear more of what this preacher had to say. He and other preachers there preached "Jesus Christ and Him Crucified;" "The Nine Gifts of the Holy Spirit;" The Nine Fruits of the Spirit;" "Spirit, Soul, and Body;" "The Healing Ministry of the Lord Jesus Christ;" and other great things, but most of all, "How to Have Faith in God."

After moving my membership to Word of Faith, the zeal of God was still in me. I join the usher staff one Wednesday night soon after joining. It was considered a megachurch that seated four to five thousand, with eight thousand on the roll. When joining the ushers, I told the director my qualifications. He seemed very pleased and positioned me in the center aisle near the pulpit. At the first church that I was a member of, the pastor appointed me his pulpit usher, so I was familiar with the duty, but was not asked at this church. Sunday mornings I was placed in the balcony, which was nice. I still had a great zeal for God, and I continued to serve well and was very faithful. I prayed that God would allow me to serve on the floor, center aisle, Sunday mornings.

As it turned out, Pastor Tilton had requested that Jim Baker would allow Word of Faith (WOF) to have prime time, Sunday mornings, ten to twelve noon on PTL. Jim Baker removed himself from prime time and allowed us at WOF to have prime time. When that happened, the president of all ushers, nights and mornings, came to the balcony where I was stationed and requested that I serve on the floor, center aisle, near the camera. Jim Bakers telecast, PTL, was nationwide. So now I would not only be serving on floor, center aisle, before all these people, most of which were white, some very wealthy, but also before the entire nation.

This was a culmination of all the prayers that were prayed. The Lord was still answering prayer daily, or doing something in my life every day to let me know that He was with me, but this request topped every prayer prayed.

While attending WOF in the early days, every morning, 5:30 or 6:00 a.m., I would wake up to Southwest Radio Church with David Webber. The program that really got my attention was when the daughter of Cecil D. DeMille was being interviewed. She had been married to Charleston Heston, who was very famous because of the movie *Ten Commandments*. He was Moses.

Every morning I heard some great teaching or testimony. The teaching that really stood out was "When the Russian Bear Comes Down from the North to Attack the Tribe of Judah." The other testimony that really got my attention was the lady that got involved deeply in witchcraft, almost lost her life and became a minister.

Not only did I have a great zeal to serve God and His people and know more about the church of the Living God, but I had (and still do) a hunger for God's Word. I could not get enough. I listened to your great teachings along with Dr. J. Vernon McGee early mornings, went to church Sunday mornings, Sunday evenings, Wednesday nights, listened to the radio in the car on my way home from work. I could not get enough.

God's Word, Christ speaking, promises "he that hungers and thirsts after righteousness shall be filled" and that "they are blessed." Well, as it turned out, we at WOF not only were on television Sunday mornings, but also we began coming together with about fifteen to seventeen hundred other churches over satellite. We began the "Satellite Seminar" the first Sunday, Monday, Tuesday, and Wednesday nights of each month, September through May. It was like going to Bible school. Plus, there was a full Bible institute available for those who wanted to attend, which I took advantage of over audiotapes.

The Lord was feeding me really well. It is why I cannot get enough teachings from Southwest Radio Church, because we know that God will be doing great things during these last days, and Southwest Radio Church covers those teachings as well as any, better than most. I cannot get enough of God's Word regarding end-time events.

Thank God for your ministry. I have not heard you on radio for a long time, but I still get your monthly newsletter. And I am still being blessed by you. It was the early eighties that I began listening to Southwest Radio Church, and it is a great blessing for God to have kept you in my heart over all these years. Thank God for you. Because of the changing of the stations on radio, I could not find you. You may have been taken off the air in Dallas, and I could never find you on air in Temple, Texas. Please consider KTON radio in Belton, seven miles from Temple, also its county seat. God's people need your ministry here in Central Texas. I believe they would really appreciate it. I have continued to order your tapes over the years: "The

Russian Bear," "The Constellation of the Stars," and others. Recently I have acquired tapes such as "The New World Disorder," "The Occult Invasion of America," and "Entertaining Spirits Unaware" and books such as *Prince Charles, The Sustainable Prince, The Anti-Prophets, The United Nations' Global Straitjacket,* and *Foundational Documents of the New World Order.* I pray for your ministry daily.

After serving two full years at WOF, a minister from another church moved his and his family's membership to our church. He began working on staff as an assistant minister. He also taught Sunday school. I attended his class. After attending a few of his classes, I heard him make a statement saying, "God has sent me to this church, and he is sending you to the church that I moved from." I think he also mentioned the fact that "they need you there."

He was speaking to an individual, but what he said was directed to all class members. I considered what he said, made a step of faith, and moved my membership to that Assembly of God church. I still had a great zeal for God's work. I joined the usher staff, and again the Lord let me know that he was with me. There is a special gift that comes with ushering if one puts his whole heart in it. The graceful hand signs and such. So much so you get the attention of all that are around you. God bless me with that. Even ministers on the pulpit took notice.

After joining the ushers, the pastor called a church meeting on Saturday regarding starting "Home Bible Studies." He assigned a church assistant minister as pastor over all Bible studies, a Care Pastor over each home and a Care Group Leader to teach the class. Care Pastors only supervised. I was first a Care Group Leader, but no one attended, so I was assigned to another home as a Care Pastor. God had opened another great door for me. It was exciting. This was another mega church, and also predominantly white, that seated three to four thousand. Before being assigned as Care Pastor, I enrolled in a two-year Bible school there at our church, Calvary Institute, which I completed with perfect attendance. God was still feeding me His Word. Sunday mornings and evenings were not enough.

Dr. Hutchings, after serving two full years at that church, I would now face the greatest test since my conversion. I had served at WOF from February 1983 until spring of 1985, and I had served at the Assembly of God church from spring of 1985 until after August of 1987, the month that I announced my retirement at Texas Instruments, to do Christian volunteer work and go into the ministry.

August 1, 1987, walking down the hallway, I was going to my desk and noticed that people that I knew began avoiding me, going to the other side of the hall when they saw me coming. I did not know what was going on. I knew that I had not faced this thing before, while growing up. My family in Cameron, Texas, was well thought of, because of my grandmother. When moving to Temple to live with my mother, I never got into any kind of trouble with the city law enforcement or at school or any other place. I was well thought of and liked by most. My friends were respectable and liked spending time with me. For me, Alvin Ervin, to be shunned was not to be considered. A lady coworker, white, approached me and said, "I have been blackballed before also."

I still did not know what was going on. There was no reason for me to be "black balled," I thought to myself. I did continue to trust God.

I moved my membership back to WOF and continued to seek God and to learn all that I could regarding what was happening. I knew my reputation was at stake. My name had always been well thought of. My grandmother would continually tell us (all eight grandchildren), "When I tell someone I'm going to do something, I'm going to do it. My word is my bond." She told us, "Do what you say you are going to do. If you tell someone you are going to do a thing, then do it." She preached and fussed at us every time we did something wrong. She also showed much love and concern for us. She taught us not to spend much time at other folks' houses so neighbors would not have anything to talk about. She told us as kids, "Never go into beer taverns, those places are for grown-ups, and never stay out late at night. Too much is going on in the world, you should be at home."

I believe those things said carried my family far. It surely helped me in life. And she always told us, "Do unto others as you would have them do to you." And now I am faced with this reputation wrecking and travesty coming against my name. The one thing that caused me to give my life to the Lord Jesus Christ was a $16.21 check that I had written to HEB grocery store. I received a letter from the DA's office saying, "If you do not pick up that check, I will put you in jail." It scared me tremendously. So much so the very next day I gave my heart to Christ, told Him that I could not do it alone, that I needed His help in life. I have been in the church and in the Lord ever since. Those two near-death accidents months earlier got my attention, but that letter meant much, much more.

After moving my membership back to WOF, I thought things would settle down somewhat. The senior assistant minister preached that spring Sunday, and he said, "You squandered your inheritance!" and many other mean things that were not true. (I had received an inheritance after my dad's death.) At least I did not think they were true. I could account for all of it, the less expensive suits that I purposed to buy and everything else. I think the most important controversy was some watches that I purchased.

Texas Instruments had an employee sales department that would allow employees to make purchases without paying (payroll deduction is what it was called). I saw several watches that I liked (two or three). One was thirty dollars, the others less. They looked really nice, but they were very inexpensive. I sometimes changed watches, especially for church. I probably offended some of my brother and sisters. Remember this was a white church. I'm sorry those things happened, and I told the pastor.

The fact is I never got into that kind of trouble or any kind of trouble with anyone before. That tells me that Satan had much to do with it, and the Lord allowed him to test me probably. Well, my faith is still in the Lord Jesus Christ, and I pray and believe that it always will be. Regarding payroll deduction, I did make other purchases, but I believe they were all payroll deducted and budgeted in with all other things that I needed. I believe the watches were the controversy because I already had a nice Seiko.

After those things occurred, it seems as if things in my life continued to get worse. Ladies were pulling their blouses up exposing themselves, girls in church pulling their dresses exposing themselves, people calling all times at night harassing. But to top it off, there were preachers saying things on national television that seemed to be directing their comments at me, such as "If you can't stand the heat, then get out of the kitchen," and many other negative things that were hurtful. But I kept the faith.

Sometime later, Robert Tilton preached a sermon regarding the "old and new wine skins," saying "You have to be willing to give up the old, if you are wanting to receive the new." I knew that I had prayed for God to give me favor with His people in this nation. That meant that I would have to be willing to give up my old reputation, no matter how pleased I was with who I was. Abraham had to be willing to give his son Isaac to be a father of many nations. The good news is I kept the faith, and God is helping me relinquish anything that I need to release.

Dr. Hutchings, as we approached the mid-nineties with the Tonya Harding incident, God began answering prayers in an even greater way. Please know that He never stopped answering my prayers. When I moved my membership from WOF in 1985 to serve at Calvary Temple Assembly of God Church, shortly after arriving, we had what was considered a "Day of Destiny." We were needing funds to complete a new building project. I have always wanted to be involved in these kinds of activities. All I had to give was my fifty-dollar tithe. So I prayed for God to help me. The Lord said give your tithe to the church as you should and I will bring the money in. Pastor J. Don George was live every Sunday at 10:30 p.m. I assisted on the telephones as people called in for counsel. Pastor Tilton presented Pastor George with a check for twenty-five thousand dollars. The Lord reminded me of the prayer I prayed hours earlier at church the same day. God is faithful!

You see He continued to answer prayer, but this would be much greater I think. Shortly after the Tonya Harding incident, I was led to pray for her. I would be awakened during the night finding myself saying "Bless your daughter, Father, in Jesus's name." I was also led for great mercy to pour into her life. Later, after the Oklahoma bombing crisis, Tonya Hardin recorded a song dedicated to the survivors. I believe it was because of prayer that she was led - to record and dedicate the record.

During the same time, I began praying for James Earl Ray. He had been in prison twenty-five years for assassantine my mentor and hero Dr. Martin Luther King. I asked the Lord to have mercy in his life and free him. Well, as you know he was never released, but he should have been. Christian Blacks in America should have rallied to have him released. The way that I knew God was answering my prayer, the family of Dr. King began to be interviewed. First, his wife Coretta, then his son and daughter. In the interviews, I believe all of them were asked how do they felt regarding the man that killed this great person of all time.

I believe God caused the media to seek, obtaining interview after interview. During some of those interviews, the media asked how they felt, like "Do you hate him and want him to spend the rest of his life in prison?" I don't know why Mr. Ray was not released, except knowing some things are harder to pray for than others. I am reminded of a man in one of the Gospels bringing his son to the Lord to cast out the devil because His disciples could not do the job. The Lord said, "This kind comes out only with prayer and fasting." Maybe I did not pray hard enough or continue in prayer long enough in Mr. Ray's behalf. But I could see the power of God moving in the midst of the interviews.

Well, Dr. Hutchings, a special Word came to me regarding praying for celebrities, especiallly politicians, people in the media, talk show hosts, servants in the legal-judicial system, local law enforcement, Secret Service, the FBI, CIA, the Air Force, Army, Navy, Marine Corps, and it was brought to my attention to pray for the Coast Guard also. Not only was it impressed upon my heart to pray for these people, but also to support/attend their community gatherings that they were and are so faithfully supporting. I was led to pray for and encourage movie, music, and sports celebrities. I was led to pray for Monica Seles in the early nineties at the local church that I was serving at as an assistant minister. It seemed as if there were no results, but "we walk by faith not by sight." After praying for Tonya Harding, it seems that I got a breakthrough to heaven and many things began happen. So much so I do not know where to start.

In prayer at home during the early nineties, I mentioned a comment made by Rev. Dr. Fred Price when he taught at one of our satellite seminars. He gave a testimony that a member of his church made. A lady of his church was on welfare, and after becoming a Christian, she visited their office and told the clerk to remove her name from their listing. "My God shall supply my need according to His riches in glory." I mentioned that testimony in prayer and asked God to bless all people that were poor and on welfare.

A few months later, I heard Governor Bill Clinton mention some of the same things that I had mentioned in prayer when he was campaigning for president. He said that he had already established a program for these people in his state and that it worked well. Please understand that I was raised in a very democratic family. Years earlier, I mentioned to my mother that I had voted for President Reagan because of fear for the lives of those men held hostage in the Middle East (Iran or Iraq). She looked at me as if she would disown me. She never said anything, but that look.

Later, on my job I was told Republicans were more conservative and that Christians should vote for them. I never voted for a Democrat, but I prayed for Mr. Clinton both terms to become president. I thought he would have glorified God by lifting up Christ more than he did, but we learn from our mistakes. Before Mr. Clinton became president, I began (and still do) pray for God to raise up more godly governmental leaders. Specifically, Pat Robinson, later, Jesse Jackson, and many more. I have this desire (or dream) to see Pat Robinson put away his Republican preference and Jesse Jackson put away his Democratic preference, the two of them coming together on the independent ticket and leading God's people unto righteousness. God also put Rev. Robert Tilton in my heart to lead His people. This is not only a desire or dream but a prayer.

Dr. Hutchings, as a Christian growing up in the Lord in the 1980s, Rev. Tilton invited the members of WOF to join him and Marte, his wife, in reading through the "One Year Bible" with them in the spring of 1988. As a growing Christian, I began. Since then I have worn out two King James, both hardback and paperback, an NIV, and I am working on a New Living Translation currently. I have had the NIV rebound for future studies and probably soon have both KJVs rebounded as well. I began the New Living Translation August of 2000.

Sir, in my study of the book of Jeremiah, I could see plainly that the Lord would have leaders to lead His people into righteousness, since only His leaders know the way of righteousness. I'm sure you understand what I saying.

I noticed in the second chapter, seventh verse, New Living Translation (NLT), that God told Israel, "When I brought you into a fruitful land to enjoy its bounty and goodness, you defiled my land and corrupted the inheritance I promised you." Dr. Hutchings, it seems that we have defiled our land by electing ungodly leaders, them taking prayer out of the schools and doing many other things to drive God out of this nation. Well, He is not going because the prayer of faith is still being prayed. In verse 8 it says, "The priests did not ask, 'Where is the Lord?' The judges ignored me, the rulers turned against me, and the prophets spoke in the name of Baal, wasting their time on nonsense."

Sir, it is bad enough for judges (of our legal-judicial system), rulers (at all levels, president, vice, speaker of the House, the Senate and House of Congress at the national level, the governors, and those who serve at the state level, and our mayors, council members, and all that serve at the local) to turn against God, but when the priests and the prophet (or any of the fivefold ministers, apostles, prophets, evangelists, pastors, or teachers) do not ask where is the Lord by seeking Him and standing for what is right, then the entire nation has gotten away from Him, or as it stated in this verse, "turned against God." In verse 26, it says, "Like a thief Israel feels shame only when she gets caught" and "Kings, officials, priests and prophets - all are alike in this."

Sir, the reason that I speak so harshly toward these leaders is because I love them and labor in prayer for them, their spouses, their children, and all family members, two to four to six and have at times prayed eight hours nonstop by the spirit of God. I believe a good way of knowing if the love of God is in one's heart, that individual will show mercy to his fellow man. I have heard many preachers say that they believed in the death penalty. To me that is not the love of God, nor is it mercy. Those people are put in prison and will be there forever if they are allowed to live.

Upon my new birth, the Lord said to me, "Every person will need me, sooner or later." If we are not showing mercy to others when we can, what should we expect when we need God's mercy? I fear God, and a good measuring stick regarding our love for Him is that we show love to one another.

Dr. Hutchings, as I studied the entire book of Jeremiah, it seems that God is speaking to the leaders throughout the book, ministers, as well as governmental leaders, either telling them to lead His people unto righteousness, or rebuking and/or correcting them for not doing it. He also speaks to the entire nation. In verse 31, He says, "O my people, listen to the word of the Lord! Have I been like a desert to Israel? Have I been to a land of darkness? Why then do my people say, 'At last we are free from God! We won't have anything to do with Him anymore.'" It seems as if all of America has made that determination—except for the remnant. God has always had a remnant. It goes on to say in verse 33, "How you plot and scheme to win your lover. The most experienced prostitute could learn from you. Your clothing is stained with the blood of the innocent and the poor."

Dr. Hutchings, August 1, 1987, many trials came. There were (and are) weaknesses in my life that I was not delivered from when giving my life to the Lord. When one enters marriage and becomes single again, he becomes open to a sexual lifestyle that is hard to deal with. He knows how the Lord feels about it, so he struggles with it. With me it was a matter of trying to relieve myself of those sexual desires. I thank God that He did deliver me from desiring the use and viewing of pornographic (or R-rated) magazine or movie. I sensed the importance of putting those things away, and I did. There were times that I found myself in ungodly positions in certain rooms (such as motels or hotels) when away from home that caused me to compromise my walk with God, and I did view those movies, but I also prayed for God to deliver me from that location or situation, and He always did.

But becoming a Christian, I came as one very innocent, not knowing anything. I thanked God for that innocence, because it represented purity, but there were (and are) those in the church that would try to steal that innocence by means of what seems to be witchcraft, but the Lord is still with me and will bring to light all those that would come against me. He also expects me to confess my sin (or shortcomings), and I have, which is also the reason I'm confessing them to you. The innocence that is being spoken of in this verse is an innocence before God (or unto) God that represents purity (or pure in heart), and I refuse to let the devil steal it (or take) it. God will judge.

The reason I am so blessed by the book of Jeremiah, regading my first opportunity to preach gospel, it was in the Baptist church where I gave my life to the Lord and was licensed as a preacher. The Lord Jesus Christ ministered to me with great power, verses 8 and 10 of the first chapter. When He encouraged me in those verses, it was a confirmation of scriptures He had previously strengthened and encouraged me in Joshua 1:5–9.

Again, God is calling His nation back to Him in Jeremiah 4:1: "Come back to me says the Lord." "If you will throw away detestable idols and go astray no more, and if you will swear by my name alone, and begin to live good, honest lives and uphold justice, then you will be a blessing to the nations of the world, and all people will come and praise my name."

Dr. Hutchings, I dream of seeing other nations being greatly blessed by our goodness and the goodness of our leaders, and I do pray that our leaders will turn their heart to God, or that He will raise and install more godly leaders. We are a city sitting on a hill for all nations to see and partake of the goodness of God.

Dr. Hutchings, now allow me to direct the attention of this letter to you and the American people (America in particular).

In chapter 4, verse 3, God tells His people to "plow up the hard ground of your hearts! Do not waste your good seed among thorns. Cleanse your minds and hearts before the Lord," by calling on the name of the Lord Jesus Christ, America. Or by going to church or by calling Southwest Radio Church asking "what must I do to be saved?" God will help you.

I want this letter/book published and to reach the hands of every leader, college and high school student in America. They should know that Christ will help them with any problem.

In the third verse of chapter 5, it says the Lord is looking for honesty. It says, "You struck your people, but they paid no attention. You crushed them, but they refused to turn from sin. They are determined, with faces set like stone; they have refused to repent."

Then said Jeremiah (or Alvin Ervin, or George W. Bush), "But what can we expect from the poor and ignorant? They don't know the ways of the Lord. They don't understand what God expects of them. I will go and speak to their leaders. Surely they will know the Lord's ways and what God requires of them." But leaders, too, had utterly rejected their God.

Verse 13 states, "God's prophets are wind bags full of words with no authority." And when the people of America ask "Why is the Lord our God doing this to us?" you must reply, "You rejected Him" (by taking prayer out of schools) "and gave yourselves to foreign gods" by serving them on Sunday, the Lord Day, playing golf, boating, watching the Dallas Cowboys, and anything else you can do to serve man. Remember, America, all the world is looking at you, but if you turn to God, they will be looking to you. "Come back to me," says the Lord, "I love you."

In verse 21, "Listen, you foolish and senseless people—who have eyes but do not see, who have ears but do not hear," says the Lord. "Do you have no respect for me?" (Or fear?) "Why do you not tremble in my presence? I, the Lord, am the one who defines the ocean's sandy shoreline an everlasting boundary that the waters cannot cross. The waves may toss and roar, but they can never pass the bounds I set." "Come back to me," says the Lord, "I love you."

In verse 23, My people, says the Lord, "have stubborn and rebellious hearts. They have turned against Me and have chosen to practice idolatry. They do not say from the heart, Let us live in awe of the Lord our God, for He gives us rain each spring and fall, assuring us of plentiful harvests. Your wickedness has deprived you of these wonderful blessings. Your sin has robbed you of all these good things."

In verse 30, "A horrible and shocking thing has happened in the land—the prophets give false prophecies, and the priests rule with an iron hand. And worst yet, my people like it that way! But what will you do when the end comes?"

Luke 12: 35 says, "Be dressed for service and well prepared, as though you were waiting for your master to return from the wedding feast. Then you will be ready to open the door and let Him in the moment He arrives and knocks." "There will be special favor for those who are ready and waiting for His return. I tell you, He himself will seat them; put on an apron, and serve them as they sit and eat. He may come in the middle of the night or just before dawn. But whenever He come there will be special favor for His servants who are ready." He (the Lord Jesus Christ) is standing at the door of your heart, America. Please let Him in, and He will come into your heart and be your best friend, your Lord and master (NLT).

Jeremiah 6:10 says, "To whom can I give warning? Who will listen when I speak? Their ears are closed, and they cannot hear. They scorn the word of the Lord. They don't want to listen at all. So now I am filled with the Lord's fury. Yes, I am weary of holding in!"

"I will pour out my fury over Jerusalem, even on children playing in the streets, on gathering of young men, and on husbands and wives and grandparents. Their home will be turned over to their enemies, and so will their fields and their wives. For I will punish the people of this land, says the Lord."

"From the least to the greatest, they trick others to get what does not belong to them. Yes even my prophets, and priests are like that! They offer superficial treatments for my people's mortal wound. They give assurances of peace when all is war. Are they ashamed when they do these disgusting things? No, not at all—they don't even blush! Therefore, they will lie among the slaughtered. They will be humbled beneath My punishing anger," says the Lord.

I believe we were warned, America, when He allowed the killings of our children and teacher at Columbine High School for removing prayer from our schools in the 1960s. I believe He is getting weary of holding His fury in, but I do believe He is holding it in because He loves us. Let's make Him proud and be pleased with us by turning to His Son, Jesus Christ.

We have allowed nations to bring their gods here, Buddha, Islam, Hinduism, and many others. Please remember, American people. People from other nations have always wanted to come to this land to make it their home because of the blessing that God gave us. He's caused us to prosper. We know in this nation we have many freedoms, one being freedom of religion. But it is God who gave us the freedoms we have because of our faith in His Son.

Even before our Founding Fathers founded this nation, it was settled by Pilgrims, a group of English Puritans who founded Plymouth Colony in 1620, who wanted to be able to worship and serve God Almighty through faith in His Son, the Lord Jesus Christ, without bowing a knee to no other gods, including the king of England. Thus, they left England, came to the new land, which we know to be the US of A. And from the very beginning of the settling of our nation, there were great problems, and with each problem the people of this nation came together to seek God's help and blessings through faith in our Lord Jesus Christ. We know that for many years God's people longed for the coming of the savior of the world, and when He arrived, His people did not receive Him, but the Gospel was made available for all nations, and the Pilgrims, our Founding

Fathers, and all the nation have rejoiced in that fact since the very beginning.

While I am most interested in the study and also the sharing with others the godly heritage of our nation, what concerns me most is why we have to continue being a godly nation and in days to come seeking our God with all sincerity of heart and with much faith.

I am a student of eschatology (end of the world), and the Bible says in the last days the entire earth will come under one world ruler. One man, the Antichrist, and his false prophet will try to rule the whole world as he set his seat in Jerusalem to deceive the Jewish race and all the world. For seven years he will deceive the world. The Bible says no one will be able to buy or sell (food or anything else) except if they have the mark of the beast on their forehead or on their right hand. The Bible also says anyone taking that mark will spend all eternity in the lake of fire (or hell).

The seven-year period of which is referred is called the tribulation. The word *tribulation* means great misery or distress as from oppression or deep sorrow. Because of the Antichrist (also referred as the beast), the entire earth will be under much oppression and he will bring deep sorrow. The last three and a half years of this seven-year period is referred to by some people as the Great Tribulation, which means the oppression and sorrow will be intensified by the Antichrist. You do not want to be on earth during that time. Our Heavenly Father has provided a way of escape through His Son. The Bible says, "Anyone that call on the Name of Lord" (Jesus) "shall be saved." Before the tribulation enters the earth, the body of Christ (all Christian people) will be supernaturally taken out of the earth by the Lord Jesus Christ. The term is called the Rapture of the Church.

Before the Rapture occurs, the Antichrist will bring the world in its entirety into a one-world government so that he can govern or rule the world himself. And Almighty God is going to allow him to do this for a brief period of time, which is the tribulation.

We know the Lord is going to allow the devil or the Antichrist, which means Satan or the devil incarnate. (This man will be wounded in his head and die. Satan will raise him from the dead.) God is going to let him rule during this period, and he is going to bitterly mistreat God's people. But it will come to an end. And we in Christ will rule and reign with the Lord for a thousand years after the Antichrist is taken out of the way. We will enter the millennial reign of the Lord Jesus Christ. The Bible also says that Christ will forever rule and reign after this period.

Again, before all these things occur, the Antichrist and the false prophet will have to bring the entire earth into "one world order" (another term you will hear quite frequently during these last days), and Satan has begun this work: the internet and the European euro is the evidence. Each nation has always had its own currency. But now the nations in Europe have come under one currency. The Bible says the entire earth will come under one world currency. Yes, the US, Canada, and Mexico as well—all nations. But the Lord Jesus Christ has told us to occupy until He comes (Luke 19:13). That means do His work until He gets back.

God gave this nation to Christian people. I love Indian people (I wanted to date an Indian girl when growing up), but I believe the Lord took this nation from the Indian to give it to Christians. I pray that the Indian race, the Native Americans, will come to a saving knowledge of the Lord Jesus Christ, and I believe they will because we are praying for them. The Bible says the earth is the Lord's and the fullness thereof and all those that dwell upon it. So we know He loves our red-skinned brothers, but He wants all of us to worship, praise, and serve Him. The Indians did not.

In Joshua 3:10, it says, "Hereby ye shall know that the living God is among you, and He will without fail drive out from before you the Canaanites, and the Hittites, and the Hivites, and the Perizzites, and the Girgashites, and the Amorites, and the Jebusites" and allow me, Alvin Ervin, to say any other nation or race that is not serving Him. I do not think there is another race on earth that has suffered as blacks, except the Jews. But if it took blacks going through all that they have in this nation to come to know Christ Jesus, then I am glad and thankful that it happened. I love you, Indians. Do you believe it? There is much to do in this nation. Give your life to the Lord and come join us. We're speaking of good against evil.

Studies show us that the Supreme Court took prayer and the study of the Bible out of our schools in 1962 to 1963. But before we deal with this issue and it was done without just cause, we first want to go back to the very beginning.

Let us look at our heritage. Is it a godly one? We know that it is. We will expound upon information given by David Barton and WallBuilders. WallBuilders is an organization dedicated to restoring "America's religious, moral, and Constitutional foundations." David Barton is the founder of WallBuilders.

Our Christian history tells us that the fifty-five Founding Fathers were Christian men, and many of them were evangelical, which means they preached the Gospel or shared the good news of the Lord Jesus Christ. In an 1856 Maryland history textbook, it states the French and Indian War, in 1754–1763, which was twenty years before the American Revolution. George Washington was twenty-three years of age. The war was between the French and British because of land along the Ohio and Mississippi Rivers. The Americans sided with the British, and most of the Indians sided with the French. The British sent twenty-three hundred handpicked veteran troops to defeat the French.

George Washington took one hundred buckskins (such as Davy Crockett, Daniel Boone, Jim Bowie) and joined the British. Seven miles from the fort where George Washington had joined twelve hundred of the troops, the French and Indians ambushed George Washington, General Braddock (the leader of the British troops), and thirteen hundred men. In July 9, 1755, 714 men lost their lives. Only thirty of the French and Indians were killed. George Washington was a colonel and one of eighty-six officers in that Army. Christian history tells us he was the only officer left alive. Several horses were shot from under him, several bullet holes were found in the jacket he wore during the fight, but none of them touched him. (Psalms 91:7 says, "Though a thousand shall fall at thy side, and ten thousand at thy right hand, but it shall not come near thee".)

George Washington wrote a letter to his family shortly after that battle that says, "By the all-powerful dispensation of providence," (or God) "I have been protected beyond all human probability or expectation; for I had four bullets through my coat and two horses shot from under me." Washington openly acknowledged that God was with him. If we love the Lord, we need to tell someone.

We are told our students are now being taught our Founding Fathers were atheists, agnostics who did not acknowledge God at all. While this is hearsay, we would like to clear the record.

Consider this statement by John Adams (our fourth president): "The general principles on which the fathers achieved independence were . . . the general principles of Christianity . . . I will avow that I then believed, and now believe, that those general principles of Christianity are as eternal and immutable as the existence and attributes of God." In this statement he is referring back to George Washington and the Founding Fathers' beliefs and passing on those beliefs as well as his own. Stating that the Christian principles as eternal (Existing forever. God has always protected this nation and all its people. His promise to us is that He always will, forever, if we continue to love and serve Him). John Adams is saying the Fathers gained our independence (our freedom). As a black person, I know what it is to gain freedom. I am thankful for all the free rights we have in this nation and that we are not under the dictates of Great Britain or France or any other nation that would try to rule us.

John Adams and some of our other Founding Fathers words were published in the American Tracts Society Tracts. (Christian Tracts are little pamphlets or a small booklet new converts and other Christians pass out to share the Gospel.)

In 1690, the first textbook was printed in America. It was called *The New England Primer* and introduced in Boston. It was used until 1900. It was considered a first-grade reader. It started with the alphabet to show students how to make one-, two-, and three-letter syllables and put those syllables together to make words. Then later they returned to the alphabet and attached a phrase to each alphabet. Each of those phrases were verses taken directly out of the Bible:

A. *A* wise son makes a *glad* father, but a foolish son is the heaviness of his mother.

B. *Better* is a little with the fear of the Lord than great treasure and trouble therewith.

C. *Come* unto Christ all you who labor and are heavy laden and He will give you rest.

It continued throughout the alphabet in this manner.

John Quincy Adams was a product of the above Christian teaching, and at fourteen years of age, he received a congressional diplomatic appointment overseas to the Court of Catherine the Great in Russia as secretary to an ambassador. He went on to serve as foreign ambassador under two presidents. He served secretary of state, a United States representative, a United States senator, and the sixth president of the United States.

In a speech on July 4, 1837, John Quincy Adams asked the crowd a question that he answered. The question was, "Why is it that, next to the birthday of the Savior of the world, your most joyous and most venerated festival returns on this day?" He answered, "Is it not that, in the chain of human events, the birthday of the nation is indissolubly linked with the birthday of the Savior?" He is telling us that you cannot separate the two, Christ's birthday and the birthday of this nation, because we have depended so much on the Lord Jesus Christ. Adams went on to say that it formed a leading event in the progress of the Gospel dispensation? Is it not that the Declaration of Independence first organized the social compact on the foundation of the Redeemer's mission upon earth? That it laid the cornerstone of human government upon the first precepts of Christianity? And on he continued for sixty pages. Here John Quincy Adams was stating the biggest victory that we won in the American Revolution was the Christian principles and civil government would be tied together in what he called an "indissoluble bond." The correct definition for that word is to melt together. Our Christian faith and the civil government of which we have inherited should be melted together.

John, our first chief justice of the Supreme Court and one of three men most responsible for the Constitution, declared, "Providence has given to our people the choice of their rulers, and it is the duty—as well as the privilege and interest—of our Christian nation to select and prefer Christians for their rulers." This gentleman was saying that we should select *only* Christian leaders as our rulers. Our Supreme Court should not have taken prayer and the study of the Bible out of our schools in 1962–1963. They did not have that right. It tells us the kind of men they were. Had they been Christian they would not have taken those very needed devotions out of our schools. We should consider suing the Supreme Court for not adhering to the rules of the justice system. They did not use any precedents when they abolished prayer and the Bible, as if they had the power to go above the laws of the land.

George Washington's Farewell Address was so vital to our educational system. It was a separate textbook for over a hundred years. He explained, "Of all the dispositions and habits which lead to political prosperity, religion and morality are indispensable supports. In vain would that man claim the tribute of patriotism, who should labor to subvert these great pillars."

Mr. Washington was saying you should not consider yourself patriotic if you labor to subvert these two great pillars. He's stating that religion and morality led us to political prosperity. The whole world has been watching us to see how we get things done. Since the sixties we have begun to decline in all areas that made us great. George Washington said that religion and morality are great pillars. We in Christianity considers the Lord Jesus Christ our great foundation (or pillar). The Bible says He is the only one that can govern the entire earth. It says in Isaiah 9:6–7, "For unto us a child is born, unto us a son is given and the government shall be upon His shoulder and His name shall be called Wonderful, Counsellor, The mighty God, The everlasting Father, The Prince of Peace. (v 7) Of the increase of His government and peace there shall be no end, upon the throne of David (in Jerusalem), and upon His Kingdom, to order it, and to establish it with judgment and with justice from henceforth even forever. The zeal of the Lord of host will perform this."

Here it is saying the government shall be on His shoulder. His shoulder is the only one that can carry the weight of the whole world because the Bible also says, "He a Solid Rock, a Sure Foundation" (which refers to that pillar George Washington is speaking of). Washington is saying Jesus Christ (which is where we get our religion and morality) has carried this nation upon His Shoulder to ensure that political prosperity that we gained until 1962–63. The Antichrist and false prophet empowered by Satan is going to deceive the people and try to bring peace and govern the world, but that will only last for seven years, because the beast, Antichrist, is going to wear God's people out, the Bible says, and Jesus Christ is going to bring his evil work to an end.

The Word of God declares Christ will be called the Mighty God, the Everlasting Father, and the Prince of Peace, and that His kingdom will have no end. Christ is the only one that can bring peace, now and always, and His kingdom will last forever.

Our Founding Fathers have delivered unto us a system of government that is enjoyed with unprecedented success. We've been very successful under our form of government. Simply because they trusted God. Many other nations went through revolutions during the same time that we did. Since then France had gone through six more, and Italy had gone through fifty more since then. Jesus Christ is our keeper, and He has kept this nation secure for two hundred years without having to change our form of government one time. There is no better form than "In God We Trust." Democracy helps, but it is Him helping us to resolve all issues in a democratic way.

Consider what sources our Founding Fathers acquired their ideas from that produced such a long governance of our nation. This question was asked by political science professors at the University of Houston. They believed they could determine the source of the Founding Fathers' idea if they could collect writings from the Founding era to see whom the Founding Fathers were quoting. The researchers assembled 15,000 writings from the era of the Founding Fathers and searched those writings. That effort spanned over a ten-year period. They isolated 3,154 direct quotes made by the Founding Fathers and identified the sources of those quotes. The researchers discovered that the Founding Fathers quoted Baron Charles de Montesquieu most often at 8.3 percent. They discovered that Sir William Blackstone was second at 7.9 percent. And John Locke was third at 2.9 percent.

Surprisingly enough, the researchers discovered that the Founding Fathers quoted the Bible four times more often than Montesquieu, four times more often than Blackstone, and twelve times more often than Locke. Thirty-four percent of the Founding Fathers' quotes were taken directly from the Bible. The study was even more impressive when the source of the ideas used by Montesquieu, Blackstone, and Locke were identified. Consider if you will the source of Blackstone's ideas as an example. Blackstone's Commentaries were used by courts more than others, for one hundred years, after being introduced in 1768. The courts used Blackstone to settle disputes, to define words, and to ex-procedure.

Blackstone's Commentaries has the final word in the Supreme Court. One may ask, What was the significance source of Blackstone's ideas? Perhaps the best answer to that question can be observed through the life of Charles Finney. Finney is known as a famous Revivalis, preacher, and minister from one of America's greatest revival, the Second Great Awakening in the early 1800s. Finney in his autobiography spoke of how he received his call in the ministry. He declared having determined to become an attorney. He just, as all law students at the time, dedicated himself to the study of Blackstone's Commentaries on law. Finney noted that Blackstone's Commentaries not only provided the laws, but also provided the biblical concepts on which those laws were based. He explained during the study of Blackstone's Commentaries that he read so much of the Bible in those commentaries he became a Christian and received his call into the ministry. Finney's life story clearly identifies the major source of Blackstone's idea for law. So while 34 percent of the Founding Fathers' quotes came from the Bible, many more came from men (like Blackstone) who used the Bible to arrive at their conclusion.

Allow me to say as a minister or even as a Christian that each time one goes to the Bible, he walks away with new life, inspired to do greater things. Is it any wonder why the writers of those commentaries, our Founding Fathers and anyone else, who lives in or conduct their lives according to the Word of God?

Numerous components of our current government can be shown through these early writings who have their source in biblical concepts, such as the "three branches of government," referenced in Isaiah 33:22 (NIV), the instruction regarding tax exemption for church found in Ezra 7:24, and many other examples.

Our biblical heritage was so well understood during the early years of the nation, and the writing of our Founding Fathers were so well known, that the Supreme Court ruled in later years the Founding Fathers' intention, keeping biblical principle as the basis. For example, consider this ruling by the Supreme Court in 1892. The court said, "No purpose of action against religion can be imputed to any legislation, state or nation because this is a religious people . . . this is a Christian nation."

What would lead the court to conclude that we are a Christian nation? This was not a lengthy case. It was sixteen pages in the court record. But the court provided eighty-seven precedents. The court quoted the acts of the Founding Fathers, they quoted acts of

Congresses, they quoted the acts of the state governments, and so on. At the end of eighty-seven precedents, the court explained that it could cite many other precedents but eighty-seven was enough to conclude that we were a Christian nation. Please keep in mind the court provided eighty-seven precedents in this case.

This is very important because the courts based their decisions on precedents. To the courts it is important to go back and examine both history and rulings from previous cases so that the courts can be consistent in its present ruling. In this case of the Church of the *Holy Trinity v United States* in 1892, the courts had always and still do use precedents in their case, but no precedents were used at all when deciding to remove prayer and Bible Study from our schools. We will bring forth more information regarding this case later in these writings.

In 1844 a school in Philadelphia announced that it would teach its students morality but not religion. The case was *Vidal v Girard*. This school believed that it did not need Christianity and the Bible, that it could teach morality without these great pillars. This policy, among others, caused this case to come before the Supreme Court. Some of the justices on the court at this time had been appointed by James Madison (our second president). This was what the US Supreme Court told that school: "Why may not the Bible, and especially the New Testament . . . be read and taught as a divine revelation in the schools; its general precepts expounded . . . and its glorious principles of morality inculcated" (for impressed upon the mind repeatedly)? "Where can the purest principles of morality be learned so clearly or so perfectly as from the New Testament?" The United States Supreme Court ruled that schools would teach Christianity and the Bible, "the source of morality."

It seems that the courts today repudiate (or refuse to accept or acknowledge) rulings delivered by the Founding Fathers themselves. It is not right! It is also disrespectful!

In 1811 the court made a ruling, which was subsequent (or later) decided by the US Supreme Court. The case was *People v Ruggles*. That court declared, "Whatever strikes at the root of Christianity tends manifestly to the dissolution of civil government." This case was about an individual writing a letter striking at the Lord Jesus Christ (who is the root of Christianity). The court said, "Whatever strikes at the root of Christianity tends manifestly to the dissolution" (or dissolving or ending) of civil government. This letter was striking at the Lord Jesus Christ. The courts said, "To strike at Christ Jesus is to strike at Christianity upon which our civil laws were founded." To strike at Christianity is to dissolve or put an end to our civil laws or government. This man was "sentenced to three months in jail and a $500 fine."

Allow me to say since the very beginning of this nation, we have always needed help in getting it started in a good moral way and needed help in keeping it going strong. Other nations try to come over and rule us. We have had many wars to deal with. We decided a long time ago that we needed the Lord Jesus Christ, who is Almighty God manifested in the flesh, to help us in all of our crises, and we still need Him. Consider Columbine High. That happened because we took prayer and the Bible out of our schools. Consider the Oklahoma Bombing. According to the one who committed the act, "The FBI had done some illegal acts," such as what happened at Branch Davidian.

Investigations show that J. Edgar Hoover had much to do with the hiding of one of the greatest (if not the greatest in the eyes of blacks) presidents, President John F. Kennedy. Mr. Hoover was the head of the FBI when President Kennedy was killed. The FBI was investigated because of what happened at Ruby Ridge.

We need Christ more than ever. Satan has become subtle in the things that he does now more than ever. There is war (a severe war) going on in this nation—good against evil. It is in every system in this nation. Our school system, in law enforcement, good police people are exposing corrupt ones, bringing them to account for their misdeeds. There are wars going on in the media. There were interviews with individuals after George Hinnard ran his vehicle into the Ruby's Restaurant and shot all those innocent people. Shortly after it happened, the people that were interviewed that knew and had talked with Mr. Hinnard said that Mr. Hinnard mentioned the fact that some people (believed ladies) mistreated him. Whoever in the media tried to bring forth the truth regarding the matter was evidently hushed. We did not hear anything else.

For whatever reason, Satan used leaders it seems to silence the truth. Truth has to be brought forth so that it can be dealt with. We need God more than ever. Regarding George Hinnard, if his friends, associates, or neighbors mistreated him, they were wrong. As Christian people, we should encourage, build up, and support our neighbors because no one knows when they'll come to the end of themselves. Usually when that happens they do something stupid. I'm sorry to say.

Regarding the case in 1811, where the man generated writings that attacked the Lord Jesus Christ, if you will notice, this matter occurred not long after the First Amendment was in in place (approximately twenty years). The First Amendment never intended to separate Christian principles from government. Yet we cease not to hear the First Amendment attached to or coupled with the phrase "separation of church and state."

The First Amendment simply states Congress shall make no law respecting an establishment of religion or prohibiting the free exercise thereof. We see that neither the word *separation, church,* or *state* is found in the First Amendment. Furthermore, that phrase is found in no founding document. Most people are familiar with the phrase, but very few know its source, and those words are important for our laws, and its origin is important and should be considered regarding all matters concerning electing and running for public office. Again, the founders and above them God never intended to separate Christian principle from government. God Almighty wants good, strong leaders in office so that His people can be led into righteousness.

We should consider there are events that are going to occur in this nation and world, in the not-too-distant future. Our leaders should know what they are and how to lead us through these things. It is going to take God's help to get us through them.

We should know the history of the First Amendment. The process of drafting the First Amendment made the intent of the Founding Fathers very clear. For before they approved the final wording, the First Amendment went through nearly a dozen alterations and discussions. Those discussions recorded in the US Congressional Records, dating June 7 to September 25, 1789, clearly show the intent of the First Amendment: By it the Founding Fathers were saying "We do not want what we had in Great Britain, in our new nation (America) today." "We do not want one denomination establishing our Christian rights. We do want godly principles, but we do not want one denomination running the nation." That intent was well understood and received. For example, in a 1799 court, *Runkel v Winemiller* declared, "By our form of government, the Christian religion is the established religion; and all sects and denominations of Christians are placed on the same equal footing."

Thomas Jefferson, to whom the popular phrase "separation of church and state" is attributed, also believed as well as the other Founding Fathers that the First Amendment prevented the federal establishment of a single denomination. In a letter to Benjamin Rush on September 23, 1800, he stated, "President Jefferson committed himself to not allow any denomination to achieve the establishment of a particular form of Christianity."

So what is the source of this phrase?

On November 7, 1801, the Baptist of Danbury Conn. wrote Jefferson concerned that "free exercise of religion" appeared in the First Amendment. To them this implied the government had the power to regulate religious expression. They believed that freedom of religion was a God-granted, unalienable (a God-given right/freedom that no one can change or transfer) right and that the government should be powerless to restrict religious activities unless those activities caused someone to "work ill to his neighbor." Jefferson understood their concern. In his response on January 1, 1802, he assured them that the free exercise of religion was indeed an unalienable right and would not be meddled with by the government. Jefferson's letter to the Danbury Baptist Association on January 1, 1802, stated, "The First Amendment has erected a wall of separation between church and state."

Today all that is heard in Jefferson's letter is the phrase "a wall of separation between church and state" without either the context or the explanation given in the letter or its application by early courts. The clear understanding of the First Amendment for a century and one half prohibited the establishing of a single national denomination. National policies and ruling during the one-hundred-and-fifty-year period always reflected that interpretation. For example, in 1853 a group petitioned Congress to separate Christian principles from government. Their petition was referred to the House and the Senate Judiciary Committee, which investigated almost a year to see if it was possible to separate Christian principles from government.

Both the House and the Senate returned with a report. The following are excerpts from the "House Report" on March 27, 1854. The Senate was very similar.

> Had the people (the Founding Fathers), during the Revolution, a suspicion of any attempt to war against Christianity, that Revolution would have been strangled in its cradle . . . at the time of adoption of the Constitution and its amendments, the universal sentiment, was that Christianity should be encouraged, but not any one sect (denomination).

The report continued, "In this age, there is no substitute for Christianity . . . That was the religion of the Founding Fathers of the republic and they expected it to remain the religion of their descendants." Two months later the Judiciary Committee made this strong declaration: the great, vital, and conservative element in our system (the thing that holds our system together) is the belief of our people in the pure doctrines and the divine truths of the Gospel of Jesus Christ.

After the case that challenged the government in 1853, there were other challenges, but they were all unsuccessful until 1947, *Everson v Board of Education*, the court for the first time in this nation—I believe when God looked down from heaven that day He was saddened—did not cite Jefferson's entire letter but extracted eight words from it. They are "The First Amendment has erected 'a wall of separation between church and state.' That wall must be kept high and impregnable."

This was a new philosophy for the court. The courts had taken Jefferson's letter out of context, it seems, and only used eight of its words. The church believed that the court purposely began to speak about separation between church and state. After the 1947 ruling, the court continued to speak about separation between church and state, saying, "This is why the Founding Fathers wanted separation of church and state. This is their great intent." The courts continued so strongly speaking about this matter until a judge handling the *Baer v Kolmorgen* case in 1958 warned that continuing to talk about the separation of church and state would make people think it was part of the Constitution.

The courts continued to speak about separation of church and state until June 25, 1962. By this time, it was said that communists had infiltrated our nation. What would cause our courts to do what was about to happen on June 25, 1962?

When we hear of something tragic that has happened in the life of a relative or a very close friend or someone that has been very special in our lives, if he or she falls in society, doing something that you would never imagine them doing, when you hear of it, it is very disheartening. One becomes extremely saddened. You drop your head, sad, almost not knowing what to do with yourself. I've received news of special people in my life falling from grace such as Jim Baker or Jimmy Swaggart or the pastor of the mega church I attended, getting a divorce. You do not gudge them, you can't, or a relative, and I find myself withdrawing from others to be alone just to consider the matter. That becomes a very sad day for me.

In 725 BC the Assyrians laid siege to Samaria, the capital of the ten northern tribes of Israel after the separation of Judah from

Israel. In 722, three years later, that siege fell and Israel was taken into captivity. God Almighty had sent prophets and seers to warn them about turning from Him to worship and serve other gods. They received many warnings but did not heed the warnings. So God sent the Assyrians to take them captive. With all the warnings Israel received, God still always gives us an opportunity to correct matters in our lives by turning to Him asking for help, which Israel did not. It was still a sad day when Israel fell. This was the nation that God raised up for all the world to see. He parted the Red Sea when Egyptians tried to kill them, and all other nations of the world knew that He delivered in this manner. When the Philistine Army sent forth a giant named Goliath, standing approximately ten feet tall, God used a little lad named David to conquer the giant to show the entire world that He was God Almighty. David's words to Goliath when he confronted him were "You come against me with sword and spear and javelin, but I come against you in the name of the Lord Almighty, the God of the armies of Israel, whom you have defied. This day the Lord will hand you over to me, and I'll strike you down and cut off your head. Today I will give the carcasses of the Philistine Army to the birds of the air and the beasts of the earth, and the whole world will know that there is a God in Israel" (1 Samuel 17:45–46, NIV).

God had raised this nation (Israel) above all nations in the world to let all the earth know that He was God Almighty and that He had chosen and raised up Israel and set her above every nation in all the earth. Please know when that siege fell and she (Israel) was taken into captivity, that was a very sad day. God had used that nation to set a standard for all nations of the world, and Israel had let Him down by serving other gods.

Please know that it was a sad day when our court in the case of *Engel v Vitale* on June 25, 1962, delivered its first ruling, which separated Christian principles from education. The court struck down school prayer.

In the 1962 case, the court redefined the meaning and application of one word, the word "church." For 170 years before the case of *Engel v Vitale*, the court defined "church" as being a federally established denomination. (Remember the Founding Father had established the church when they declared there would be no set denomination but all denominations would be recognized by the government, and all national leaders would have acknowledged their faith that basically derived from one of those denominations.)

However, this 1962 case redefined church to mean any religious activity performed in public. Before this case, the church was involved in all walks of life, but now it would be only one activity performed in public. This was the turning point in the interpretation of the First Amendment.

Understand that what the courts were now announcing was that no longer would the First Amendment simply prohibit the establishment of federal denomination. It would now prohibit religion activities in public settings. This current doctrine of separation is a brand-new doctrine; it is not from the Founding Fathers, and it is not in any of our founding documents. Even secular sources acknowledged, recognized this policy is a recent one. Yet notice how much the American people have had to give up in recent years under this new doctrine.

School prayer was the first casualty with the redefinition of the First Amendment in the 1962 Engel case. School prayer had never been challenged before this time, for clearly school prayer had never established a national denomination and therefore had always been acceptable, but under the new definition, school prayer was definitely a religious activity in public and therefor now deemed to be unconstitutional.

The 1962 case, which now redefined the First Amendment and removed school prayer, was noticeable in a number of aspects. The 1892 case, *Church of the Holy Trinity v United States* quoted eighty-seven precedents to maintain the inclusion of Christian principles in our laws and in our institutions. The 1962 case was just the opposite. It was the first case in American history to use no precedents, *Engel v Vitale* (1962). Please consider this was also the time it was said our nation was being infiltrated by communists. This means the Supreme Court removed school prayer without using any precedents, and no one challenged what was happening.

The court quoted zero previous legal cases, and without any historical or legal base, the court announced, "We will not have prayer in schools anymore." That violates the Constitution. A brand-new direction was taken in America.

Within a twelve-month period of time, in two more cases in 1963, the court had not only removed prayer but also Bible reading, religious classes, and religious instructions. This was a radical reversal. A book from 1946 illustrates this. This particular book entitled *Bible Study Course, New Testament,* from Dallas High School, September 1946, Bulletin No. 170, authorized by Board of Education, April 23, 1946, printed in the Dallas Public Schools Printshop, Dallas, Texas. The introduction further states this was a credit course toward graduation in Dallas High Schools.

What had happened in the 1962–63 rulings were a radical reversal of national policy prior to that point. It was in the *Abington v Schempp* and the *Murray v Curlett* decisions in June 17, 1963, that the court not only reaffirmed the ban on school prayer but also banned school Bible reading. Recall that in the brief survey already presented, the

Founding Fathers relied on the Bible, early textbooks quoting the Bible, and used it as part of the alphabet, and earlier Supreme Court ruled that a school must teach religion and the Bible. Therefore, what possible bases can the 1963 court justify its ruling to stop the use of the Bible in schools?

The court always explains its decision in written form. That 1963 case was no different. If one examines that case in a law library, he or she would find why the Bible had to be removed from schools. In its written decision, the court noted that "if portions of the New Testament were read without explanation, they could be and . . . had been psychologically harmful to the child." For 170 plus years, there had not been this problem or any other problem with our students reading the Bible in schools. This matter should be thoroughly investigated and all details brought before the entire nation. God loves His people, and a child being harmed by reading God's Word is unnatural and unlike His nature. The students should seek help from their teachers or parents if they are having problems with understanding the Bible, just as they would do with any other subject. They are learning, remember, and they will need help. Grown-ups even seek help when they do not understand certain parts of the Word of God. I'm a Sunday school teacher, and I've seen it happen many times.

Regarding this case, it was the second time in a year that a case was lacking both historical and legal precedent. Again the court simply made a new announcement of policy: "No more Bible reading in schools." The court continued to extend the boundary outward. In 1965 in *Reed v Van Hoven*, the court allowed prayer over lunch in school as long as no one could tell it was a prayer. They were not allowed to say words or move their lips, but they could pray if no one knew that they were praying. In 1967 in *De Kalb v De Spain*, the court took a four-line nursery rhyme used by a K-5 kindergarten class and declared that nursery rhyme unconstitutional. The court explained although the word *God* was not used, if someone were to hear the rhyme, he might think it was talking about God, and that would be unconstitutional. This trend continued in case after case, year after year.

In one year alone, three cases made the courts, challenging the rights of the students to see the *Ten Commandments* while at school. The Supreme Court accepted the *Stone v Graham* from Kentucky where a copy of the Ten Commandments was hanging in the hallways of the school. The court acknowledged that the Ten Commandments were passive displays. That is, they only hung on the wall like a picture of George Washington. They were a part of any class or curriculum. They just hung there. A student could observe them if he or she wanted to. If not, they did not have to. Yet notice the court ruling under the redefined First Amendment. The court said if the posted copies of the Ten Commandments are to have any effect at all, it will be to induce the schoolchildren to read, meditate upon, perhaps to venerate and obey, the Commandment . . . (which) is not a permissible . . . objective.'

Please allow me to say some decisions can be derived from using a little common sense. The court is saying "the students may meditate upon, perhaps to venerate (or to worship), and obey, the Commandments." That is the general idea. Remember Columbine High. Perhaps if students had "meditated, venerated (worship, revered) and obeyed," we would not have a teacher and all those students dead. One of the Ten Commandments is "Thou shalt not kill." If a student took those words to heart . . .

I read my Bible daily, meditate on what has been studied, and pray that God helps me to think (meditate) on so that I will not be such a monster in life. Again, common sense.

As a child growing up in the fifties, I watched the weekly TV show entitled "Wagon Train." In one viewing, there was this man and wife moving west, a part of the Wagon Train. Many covered wagons made this train. This particular man's wife was expecting. She began having complications while in labor, and the husband was told both could not live. He made the choice for his wife to live. Common sense tells one if he or she has to make a choice it would surely be the baby. But common sense tells you or should tell you to not murder an innocent baby by having an abortion.

The main factor is neither the law nor the government had any say in matters in the early days of our nation, and we should be responsible enough, and they should not have any say in the matters now. Students should be able to pray and read/study their Bibles in school. Common sense!

When the court declares something unconstitutional, it is inferring that our Founding Fathers, the men who drafted the Constitution, would have opposed it. Yet notice what James Wilson had to say about this matter. James Wilson was a signer of the Constitution, an original justice on the Supreme Court, and coauthor of America's first legal Commentaries on the Constitution. Certainly he's qualified to speak on the intent of the Constitution. He explained, "Human law must rest its authority ultimately upon the authority of that law which is Devin . . . far from being rivals or enemies, religion and law are twin sisters. Indeed, these two sciences run into each other. The divine law . . . forms an essential part of both." Our Founding Fathers were clear about the important and inseparable role that religious principles played in the life of the nation.

The entire controversy over God and religious activities and teachings in school had begun with a twenty-two-word prayer in the *Engel v Vitale* case in 1962. That twenty-two-word prayer, the prayer that led to the removal of all prayers from American schools, simply said, "Almighty God, we acknowledge our dependence upon Thee, and we beg Thy blessings upon us, our parents, our teachers and our country." This prayer that acknowledges God was a bland prayer. It was so bland that, eight years later, when a court was discussing that prayer, it described that prayer as a "to whom it may concern" prayer.

This special prayer should return to the schools as soon as possible. This prayer acknowledged God once. That one acknowledgement of God is the same number of times in the Pledge of Allegiance. The Declaration of Independence acknowledges God four times. Why should the students not pray to the same God that is mentioned in the Declaration of Independence four times? Again, that prayer should return to the classroom. And concluded in the name of Jesus Christ our Lord.

Since this simple prayer acknowledged God, the court continued to find - what percentage of the nation believed in God. In the 1963 case of *Abington v Schempp*, the court reported that only 3 percent of the nation did not believe in religion or God. Ninety-seven percent of the nation believed in God. Nevertheless, the court took another first. It sided with the 3 percent against the 97 percent. This nation is still a democracy (the majority rules). It has always been that way. Some leaders say that we are a Republic. I believe each person in this nation wants his or her voice to be heard rather than trusting an elected official, especially when they are not honoring their promises and honoring the Lord Jesus Christ.

Regarding this issue, this was the first time in the history of our nation that 3 percent had become majority. In the past, 3 percent has always been the minority, but now the philosophy of the 3 percent would be the philosophy under which the 97 percent would have to conduct its affairs.

The four categories in that prayer which petitioned God's blessings were the following:

1. "upon us" (students)
2. "our parents" (families)
3. "our teachers" (schools)
4. "our country" (nation)

There are a number of court cases readily available that show that, until 1962 to 1963, the courts consistently ruled using biblical principles and following biblical guidelines in all four of those areas. For example, in Ana of families, even in twentieth-century divorce cases, the courts explained that divorce was allowed for very few reasons, and that was because the Bible only allowed very few reasons. The court pointed out that it had not created the family. God did. Thus, it did not have the right to regulate something it had not created. The courts even went into a Bible lesson, explaining that "in the beginning, God made Adam and Eve." God made the first family, and the courts continued through a history of God's dealing with the family, concluding that since it was God who created the family, the courts would use His rules in dealing with it.

The same policy not only held true regarding the families but also the court's ruling on the nation, schools, and students as well. But in 1962–63 the Supreme Court reversed that position and announced that those rules and policies caused psychological damage. Did the court's decision to change national policy and to separate God's principles from its ruling have an effect? Let's consider each of the four categories, beginning with students. That which occurred with students following the removing of religious principles was perfectly predicted by George Washington in his farewell address when he said, "And let us with caution indulge the supposition that morality can be maintain without religion. Whatever may be conceded to the influence of refined education on mind . . . reason and experience both forbid us to expect that national morality can prevail in exclusion of religious principle."

Washington warned that to remove religious principles would be to lose national morality. Consider the accuracy of his warning. Decades prior to 1962–63 birth rates for teen girls unmarried had remained relatively stable; however, with the court's separation of religion principles from students in our schools, birth rates for unwed girls have now increased every year since 1962–63. This statistic indicates birth rates for high school girls, but birth rates for girls ten through fourteen years of age have increased 553 percent since the removal of religious principles.

This is a strong collation (or comparison). Perhaps this is coincidental but is both complete and striking. It is further significant to note that every moral measurement for students brakes violently upward with the separation of religious principles from the lives of students in 1962–63.

Consider this category: Sexual Transmitted Diseases: High school students have increased 226 percent; for students ten to fourteen years old sexual transmitted diseases have increased 257 percent; for students engaging in premarital sexual activity sixteen years of age have increased 365 percent; students involved in premarital sexual activity at seventeen years of age have increased 271 percent; students engaging in premarital sexual activity at eighteen years old is up 208 percent. Again, each of these categories was showing overall declines prior to 1962–63, but with the first ever separation of religion principles from students, a violent upturn occurred in every age group of all our students regarding every moral measurement. George Washington was correct: "Reason and experience both forbid us to expect that national morality can prevail in exclusion of religious principle."

The next category that God was acknowledged in that simple prayer in which the courts had maintained the use of biblical principles prior to 1962 was that of our families. What happened when we abandoned the use of God's principles when dealing with our families (or our parents)? Consider the area of divorce. Statistically, the divorce rates had been steadily declining for years, and even decades, prior to 1962–63. Beginning in 1963, the divorce rates skyrocketed. The United States has now become number one in the world in the rate of divorce. Our divorce rate is up 117 percent. It is again striking that every measurement related to the breakup of the family statistically skyrocketed in 1963, with the separation of biblical principle from public policy. Single-parent families up 140 percent. Single parents with children are up 160 percent. Even family morality is dramatically different. Unmarried couples up 536 percent.

Again, each of these categories has been stable for years prior to 1962–63. The dramatic increase referred to the exact years that the court took godly principles from the public. For 170 years prior to 1962–63, this nation could sense God's presence within us. We sense the moving of the Holy Spirit in our lives on an individual basis, but not as a nation. It should not take the president having to declare a special day of prayer and memorial for us to come together in worship of our God. He is a good God, a loving God, and the only true and living God. All others are false, and this nation was built on the foundation of that same God who came in the manifestation of the Lord Jesus Christ, and any group serving any other god is not a true patriarch.

Remember that is why our forefathers left England so that they would not have to bow before King James or any other person or any other god. And they gave their lives for that cause, and our Founding Fathers picked up where they (the Puritans) left off and went on to establish this nation, and as a Christian one, and again, if you are not a believer of this God and are not willing to lay your life down for this nation, you are not a true patriarch.

The third category in which God's assistance was petitioned was our schools (or teachers). What happened when we barred God from our schools. The SHT text (Scholastic Aptitude Text) is a perfect indicator. The SAT test has been in our school since 1926, and in 1941 it was placed on the same scale that is used today. Prior to 1963, there were never more than two consecutive years where the scores either rose or declined. But beginning in 1963, scores plummeted for eighteen consecutive years. Scores are now so low that the Department of Education states that this is the first time in America's history that we are graduating a generation of students who academically know less than their parents did. The SHT test is the same test that their parents used. It has been the same since 1941. Yet there is nearly an eighty-point difference between the two generations.

In 1962 there was only one thousand Christian schools in the US. But when it became obvious that things like prayer, Bible reading, and the Ten Commandments would be forbidden, there was a marketed explosion in the number of religious and particular Christian schools. By 1984 the number of Christian schools had exploded to 32,000 schools. Currently, eight and one half million students (approximate 12 percent of student population) attend religious private schools. According to the board responsible for the SHT test, the scores of students of private schools are nearly eighty points higher than those of public schools, which place them at the same level of scores prior to 1962–63.

For religious private schools, it is as if no change has occurred. But for public schools, their scores are still continuing to decline. Another indicator of the impact of religious principles and religious school have had on American education is found in the academic cream of the crop. The nation's academic elite, the national merit semifinalist. These are the top .5 percent of the nation's students. According to the Department of Education 12.4 percent of the nation's students attend private religious schools. Eighty-seven point six percent attend public schools. Since 12 percent of the nation's students attend private religious schools. Religious private schools should produce 12 percent of the nation's cream of the crop, and 88 percent of the public schools should produce 88 percent of the cream of the crop, yet that is not what is occurring.

For example, in recent testing, that small group of 12.4 percent of the nation's students from private schools were producing 39.2 percent of the nation's top academic scholars. These statistics were shown to a US congressman. He looked at them and stated, "That makes perfect sense to me. When you are talking about private schools, you are talking about money." The private schools should get better grades than public schools. What he said was investigated to see if it was true.

It was found, according to the Department of Education, that "the average private school costs $2,200 per student, while the average public school costs $5,400 per student." Private schools with two-fifth the funds are proportionately turning out a percentage of academic scholars three times higher than public schools. But what is the fundamental difference between public and private school? It is not in the core curriculum. The curriculum is the same. The Silver War takes place at the same time in both schools. The basic difference is that one school utilizes religious principles and one does not, which appears to make an eighty-point difference on the SAT test.

The fourth and final category was our country. What happens in the nation when we separate religious principles from public arenas? What would happen when we tell students things like "You cannot see the Ten Commandments you might obey them," things like "Thou shalt not kill" or "steal" (consider Columbine High)? It has to have an effect on behavior. It did! Washington in yet another warning in his farewell address accurately predicted what occurred. He said, "Let it simply be asked, where is the security for life, for reputation and for property, if the sense of religious obligation deserts?"

The sense of religious obligations has deserted, and currently, there seems no security for life, for reputation, or for property. For example, consider violent crimes. After remaining statistically stable for years since the removal of religious principles in 1962, the number of violent crimes surpassed population growth by 794 percent, causing the United States to become the world's leader in violent crimes. Perhaps the best explanation for this increase was given by Thomas Jefferson who states why Christianity was the best friend to government. He explained, "The precepts of philosophy laid hold of action only . . . (but Jesus) pushed His scrutinies into the heart of man, erected His tribunal in the region of His thoughts, and He purified the waters at the fountainhead."

Where the laws says don't kill, in Matthew 5, Jesus says "Don't get angry, don't hate." Clearly if one prevents the anger, the hate, you have prevented the murder. Where the law says "Don't commit adultery," Jesus says, "Don't lust in your heart." If you control the lust, you have controlled the adultery. The Founding Fathers pointed out that only religion could stop crime before it started, because all crimes come out of the heart, and if you cannot control the heart, you cannot control the crimes. That is why Christian principles were so vital to government. Most of the Founding Fathers expressed that same understanding.

President John Adams pointed out that there was no government in the world able to make someone do what was right, or able to control those who did not wish to be controlled. President Adams explained, "We have no government armed with power capable of contending with human passions unbridled by morality and religion." He continued on by saying, "Our Constitution was made only for a moral and a religious people. It is wholly inadequate to the government of any other." The Founding Fathers believed that the Constitution works only for people with internal restraints and internal controls. For people that would use the Word of God as their standard.

We have moved away from that, and clearly the Constitution apart from religious principles is not working the way that it should, a fact evident on all the charts and statistics. Since 1962–63, the United States has undergone marked statistical reversals. Becoming the world's leader in the most unenviable categories. United States is now number one in the world in the following:

> Violent crime
> Divorce
> Teenage pregnancies (Western World)
> Voluntary abortion
> Illegal drug use
> Illiteracy (Western World)

Of all industrial nations we have the highest illiteracy rate. A White House briefing recently reported that just three years ago, seven hundred thousand students graduated from high school, who after twelve years of school were unable to read their own diplomas.

Looking at the list of categories that we now lead, Jeremiah 6:16 has some good advice. It instructs us that if we want the way of peace to "go back to the old paths, but what were the old paths?" We in the US need to seek God for our direction (or the old path).

Once the Founding Fathers had declared themselves independent of Great Britain, they immediately faced the task of establishing new state governments. Prior to the declaration, all the state governments had been British run with British Crown governors. By breaking from Great Britain, the states lost their governments. So after signing the Declaration of Independence, the Founding Fathers returned to their home states to establish brand-new state governments. Consider what the Founding Fathers, the men who had signed the documents, placed in their own state's Constitutions. For example, notice Delaware. The other states were very similar.

Every person appointed to public office shall say, "I do profess faith in God the Father, and in Jesus Christ His only Son, and in the Holy Ghost, one God, blessed forevermore, and I do acknowledge the Holy Scriptures of the Old and New Testament to be given by divine inspiration." This was not a requirement to be a church leader. This was a requirement to be a politician. A requirement set up by the Founding Fathers themselves. But notice that this requirement is consistent with the First Amendment because it did not require for someone to be from one specific denomination to hold public office. It only stated that one had to understand God's principles. That you had to understand God's Word to hold public office.

The different state Constitutions contained several common components. For example, consider Pennsylvania and Vermont Constitutions: "And each member (of the legislature), before he takes his seat, shall make and subscribe the following declaration: 'I do believe in one God, the Creator and Governor of the universe, the rewarder of the good, and the punisher of the wicked.'" In other words, a politician must acknowledge his understanding that when he left his office, he would not just answer to the voters; he would be accountable to God for what he had done wrong in office. He would answer to God Himself.

This concept of individual accountability to God is well understood. It is broadly accepted that we will answer to God in the future. The Founding Fathers, however, took this principle a step further. It was clear that an individual would answer to God. But did a nation answer to God? The Founding Fathers believed that it did.

On the floor of the Constitutional Convention, it was explained the difference between an individual accountability to God and national accountability to God. An individual answers to God in the future. But not a nation. When a nation dies, it is dead forever (unless it is Israel). Therefore, when does a nation? George Mason, the father of the Bill of Rights, explained, "As nations cannot be rewarded or punished in the next world, so they must be in this. By an inevitable chain of causes and effects, Providence punishes national sins by national calamities."

The Founding Fathers believed that God would deal with a nation now, in the present, for the stands that it takes. A nation has no other time to answer to God than the present. Perhaps this is the best explanation of why all the charts rose dramatically in 1962–63, when for the first time in the nation's history, we told our God He was no longer welcomed officially, by the people, to be our leader in public affairs of this nation. The charts simply illustrate a principle the Founding Fathers understood, believed, and discussed.

Supporting examples are found throughout the Bible. For example, the story of Elijah the Prophet in I-Kings. After he won his confrontation with the prophets of Baal on Mount Carmel, he went to God and complained, saying, "Get me out of here. I am the only one left, there is no one else who believes in you." The Lord's reply was "There are seven thousand others who have not bowed their knees to Baal." Yet what had occurred in that nation? The nation had been led by very wicked leaders, Ahab and his wicked wife Jezebel. Because of their wickedness, the wickedness of the nation's leaders (the nation of Israel, United States or any other nation) endangered the lives of the citizens. In Israel, because of King Ahab and Jezebel, God shut up the heavens, and there was no rain for three and a half years.

In the United States, because of our politicians and the Supreme Court in the 1960s, prayer and the study of the Bible was removed from the schools, God allowed the killings at Columbine High. God had to deal with the nation based on the stands of the nation. When God shut up the heavens and no rain fell for three and a half years, the righteous seven thousand suffered as much as the wicked, but the righteous were innocent. When the killings occurred at Columbine High, the entire nation was affected. And the taking of prayer and the Bible out of the schools is what caused the killings, according to the way that God deals with His people and the nation. Again, God had to deal with nation based on the stands of the nation's leaders.

This is why our Founding Fathers were so determined about keeping men in office who understood God's principles. And perhaps the most famous speech ever delivered by Benjamin Franklin, delivered Thursday, June 28, 1787, on the floor of the Constitutional Convention, Franklin reminded the delegates, "We needed God to be our friend and our ally," not our enemy. "We needed to keep God's concurring aid. If a sparrow cannot fall to the ground without His notice, is it probable that an empire can rise without His Aid?"

Franklin went on to make a strong statement that comes directly from the Word of God. "We've been assured in the sacred writing, that, 'Except the Lord build the house, they labor in vain that build it.'" And thus, Franklin called for regular daily prayer to make sure we kept God in the midst of what we were doing in the nation. Jefferson, too, understood this principle. He declared, "And can the liberties of a nation be thought secure when we have removed their only firm basis—a conviction in the minds of the people that these liberties are the gift of God? That they are not to be violated but with His wrath? Indeed I tremble for my country when I reflect that God is just; that His justice cannot sleep forever."

A nation certainly answers to God for the stands that it takes. Abraham Lincoln, during the Civil War, overheard someone in the White House state "that he hoped that God was on our side during the battle," that God was on the side of the Union. Lincoln, showing that he understood the principle of national accountability, replied, "Sir, I am not at all concerned about that, for I know the Lord is always on the side of the right. But it my constant anxiety and prayer that I and this nation should be on the Lord's side." This understanding of national accountability to God has been part of our heritage, part of our history. Our Founding Fathers understood that a nation needed to take stands that lined up with God's principles so that God's blessings and His "concurring aid," as was stated by Benjamin Franklin, could rest on the nation.

Elias Boudinot, who served as president of the Continental Congress, made a recommendation that sums up what must again happen in America. He said, "Let us enter on this important business under the idea that we are Christians on whom the eyes of the world are now turned . . . let us in the first place . . . humbly and penitently implore the aid of the Almighty God whom we profess to serve—let us earnestly call and beseech Him for Christ's sake to preside in our councils." He was saying, if you want to be a world's leader, then put Christian principles in your public affairs.

Charles Finney states, "The church must take right ground in regard to politics. Politics are a part of a religion in such a country as this, and Christians must do their duty to the country as part of their duty to God . . . (God) will bless or curse this nation, according to the course (Christian) take (in politics)."

Why is this true? Can a nation be blessed apart from God's principles? No! Where does God's principles reside? They reside in the hearts and lives of God's people. If God's people do not get involved, God's principles will not be involved. The ungodly will not run a nation with godly principles, and God cannot bless ungodly principles. That is why Christian people have to take their part in the leadership of this nation, to take their ground with God's help and lead our nation back in right standing in the eyes of all the earth, that God receives the glory that He deserves and that America may once again shine as a light for other nations. That is why the Founding Fathers were so determined to keep Christian men in office. They stressed this importance from the first Supreme Court justices to the individual state Constitutions.

Today we cannot afford to be an isolationist. We must realize that we need to get involved. God's principles do not enter any arena on their own. They enter only through God's people. Proverbs 18:1 says, "A man who isolates himself seeks his own desires; he rages against all wise judgment."

The Founding Fathers taught their young people to become leaders in the society that they were a part of by becoming a senator, or judge, a congressman, a doctor, a lawyer, a missionary or a pastor, but get out before the people so that you will be effective with God's principles. Beginning in the 1940s and '50s, we began telling of young folks "to become pastors, or missionary," but do not get involved in politics. When we began getting out, we turned the nation over to ungodly principles. We have to get involved again. We have to come to grips with the fact that separation of church and State, as we have it today, is not in the teachings of the Founding Fathers. It is not a historical teaching, and it is not a teaching of law (until recent years). We also have to realize that the current version of separation of church and state is not a biblical teaching.

We have lost ground in recent years, as we've lost our understanding of the Founding Fathers' intents and teachings. We do have a godly heritage in America. But we've been robbed, robbed by the 3 percent. Separation of church and state, as we have it today, is not a biblical teaching. It is not a teaching of our Founding Fathers, it is not a historical teaching, and it is not a teaching of law, until recent years. The 3 percent have taken away our heritage. We've lost sight of it. We have to get involved and take it back. A godly heritage is the foundation of America. And the church must take the ground that it's lost. We must take with God's help the things we've given up in recent years. We Must Get Involved.

As a child growing up in a Baptist Christian family under my grandmother, Celester Dotsey, and mother, Eddie Dotsey-Jordan, I see myself at the ages of six, eight, and ten years old praying the Lord's Prayer every night before going to bed. Sometimes our grandmother would tell us (myself, my brother, Hue and six cousins, the Moores) stories about our family in the past and of other people as well—the story of the Humble Family was very touching and effective in our lives regarding causing the fear of God to come upon us, concerning doing what was right and being careful in life. As small children, we sometimes got sleepy while listening to those stories, and when bedtime came, I would sometimes be too sleepy to say my prayer. But the next night I remember making up for the night that I missed and all other times I may have missed out of respect and reverence to our God in heaven and also telling how sorry I was for missing saying my prayers the night or other times before.

Because of those prayers I prayed as a child, I believe God protected me when moving from the small town of Cameron, Texas, to a larger city of Temple, Texas, and other kids larger than I threatening to beat me up and when moving from Temple to Dallas, Texas, as a young adult walking home at two or three o'clock in the morning on the weekend, several miles from South Dallas to South Oak Cliff being approached by people wanting me to perform very ungodly act for them and God giving me the strength to tell them "I am not made that way." Being very naive in life and regarding the ways of the world, especially in a large city, and being terrorized. As a boy growing up, I lived a very sheltered life. After growing up, and being involved in several near-death auto accidents, to walk away completely unharmed would be only by God's grace, and I believe that grace came because of those prayers prayed as a child.

Prayer needs to go back to our schools. It needs to be accompanied by the study of the Bible, and teachers should have a right to spank our children. The Bible says "If you spare the rod, you will spoil the child." They should be spanked in a very loving way. Or they should be spanked by the teachers letting them know that they love that child very much and that spanking took place to correct them only. Because of that love, that child will receive that correction and not be rebellious. Again, godliness needs to return to our schools, especially prayer and the study of the Bible, and with the permission of parents, the spanking of our children.

Again, the information used regarding own national history was taken from a video that I support entitled *America's Godly Heritage* by WallBuilders with David Barton narrating, which I obtained through Focus On the Family (then led by Dr. James Dobson, whom I honor greatly).

July 2001

To you leaders, especially the president, senators, and governors, but to all you leaders including church leaders, God says to you from the Word of God in Micah 6:8, "The Lord has already told you what is good (or right), and this is what He requires: to do what is right (or just), to love mercy, and to walk humbly with your God."

To President Bush. Know that God is with you as long as you continue to strive to do what is right, and it looks like you are putting forth a good effort. God is saying be encouraged and know that "there hath no temptation taken you but such as is common to man; but God is faithful who will not suffer to be tempted above that ye are able; but with the temptation also make a way to escape, that ye may be able to bear it" (1 Cor. 10:13).

In the past, at least once as a governor and once as president you've been tempted and have allowed the death penalty, and it should not have been. You've stood before this nation and those in Europe and declared your moral convictions. Stand firm and declare to this nation it is not right to put people to death. Rather God expects us to love (and show) mercy. "Blessed are the merciful, for they shall obtain mercy" (Matt. 5:7).

As you have stood firm to declare your moral
convictions regarding other issues; I have provided
a way of escape regarding the death penalty, 'tell the
nation it is not morally right.' That temptation and all
temptations I will (says the Lord) be faithful to provide
a way of escape for you and anyone that will call on
the name of the Lord Jesus Christ. (Rom. 10:9–10)

Our nation has slipped into sin, and it seems as if the people are
unaware of it, which includes preachers because if they were aware of
the fact, flags would be raised, marches would take place, the media
would be notified, parents would tell children to spread the news at
school, children would ask their parents to spread this knowledge at
work, and preachers would preach all the time that we as individuals
and as a nation should repent and turn to the Lord Jesus Christ. As a
minister of the Gospel, God holds me accountable to apply the Word
of God to my life as well as others.

I allow myself to serve in the ministry as a prophet because I
believe that God would have me speak the truth when its needed. The
prophets were in time past (and now) responsible for monitoring the
moral conviction of the nation and for holding the political leaders
accountable when their action violated the standards set by the
nation's real leader.

Prophets are also to confront other prophets who have gotten
away from God and priests as well.

The president has the right, said God, and should confront
corporate leaders in the nation, reinforcing the fact that all business
matters should be handled fairly (or justly).

As a minister of the Gospel, serving as a prophet, I praywhich is
one of the fivefold ministries; the other four being apostle, evangelist,

pastor, and the teacher), I have suffered many things at the hands of other ministers, leaders of this nation, the media, celebrities, and others stationed in different workplaces throughout the nation (all part of an underground network which seems to be organized by individuals using spiritual forces-), doing whatever they can to get one in trouble, to cause an individual to commit an illegal act so that they would have something to hold over that person to make that individual obey them.

In the days of old, leaders would imprison, beat, or kill the prophets (see 1 Kings 22:24–26; Matt. 23:31, 34). Now everything is done subtly, but God will judge them. This method of intimidation is extremely effective and is used to control all those who cannot be controlled legally or otherwise controlled. Lives are threatened, family members' lives are threatened, and those threats are made good. When threats are not made, acts are carried out to get one's attention to let one know - they mean business and are very serious about what action they're taking, but Jesus Christ is still the Lord of the earth and He will judge them, and I believe the time will be soon. They put temptations (like very attractive ladies,) before you and dare you look at them and then try to do everything in their power to cause an individual to yield to that temptation.

Christian people do not want to yield to sinful temptations (I've in fact ran from them), but each individual has the God-given and legal right to look at, talk to, and try to get acquainted with anyone (no matter what color) they want. I'm reminded of a time when visiting an individual at the Belton, Tx Jail. I saw a white young lady staring at me. I looked at her, and she said, "You couldn't get to me even if you wanted to." There have been many others acting the same way, but God is still the judge.

When I became a volunteering minister for JAIL ministries at the jail in Belton, Texas, to make me look unfaithful a white lady was there, I believe, to purposely tempt me in any way she could along with a couple of white gentlemen. As a result, I began having transportation problems and were not able to get to the ministry. Before that a white person driving across the parking lot of Kroger Grocery Mart in Dallas/Balch Springs, Texas, in an older model Cadillac by all purpose and intent ran into the side of my little Subaru as I drove along.

There have been countless times that I have been harassed in my job to the extent of me losing that job, or those individuals purposely causing me to be terminated: Redi-Mix Concrete, Lewisville, Texas; McClains, Temple, Texas; Temple & Belton ISD, Temple & Belton, Texas; Dallas ISD, Dallas, Texas (would not give me a pay increase). Thirteen years of harassment since retiring from Texas Instruments of which I encountered no harassment of that sort through the full nineteen years of employment there, except the last few months—that is, when it started on the job.

In time past I've opened credit accounts to obtain credit card and tried to get my life back on track, to find myself losing the job, the credit card balance rocketing from two hundred dollars (which was the credit limit) to fifteen hundred dollars. In time past the bankers in this nation would have closed the account at two hundred dollars when it was apparent the individual was having financial problems, tried to set up some kind of payment plan and the balance would not have exceeded two hundred dollars because the account would have been closed or closely watched. But the real issue is none of these problems would have occurred if problems would not have occurred on the job.

There were times when I tried to get assistance at the bank. These same people did everything possible to stop me from getting help. Thus, nothing materialized regarding the internet business and other things I needed assistance at the bank.

All groups, businesses, and individuals that I'm speaking about—I pray that God will help them to acknowledge the truth, accept a rebuke given by the love of God, ask God to forgive them, and allow Him to bless their lives by receiving the Lord Jesus Christ as savior of their lives.

George W. Bush was the president that God allowed to lead our nation. It is by His (God's) permissive will that He allowed Mr. Bush to lead. His perfect will is for Pat Robertson, minister of the Gospel, to put away his Republican political preference and Jesse Jackson, minister of the Gospel, to put away his Democratic political preference, them both come together on - an independent ticket, to show forth love between the two races that have been fighting - each other for hundreds of years, and to show forth unity between the two political parties that have been fighting against each other in the past.

Our political parties have become gods to the American people, and God, our Father, gave them to us as a way of conducting business—all systems (political, legal, judicial, banking, especially school, security—Secret Service, FBI, CIA, Air Force, Army, Navy, Marine Corps, Coast Guard), also the media, and all other sources we use to keep our nation strong. Even day and night were given to us by the Lord Jesus Christ. Night, to get our rest that keeps us strong and day to conduct our business. When the religious leaders of Christ's day came to Him to honor the day (being the Sabbath), His reply was "Sabbath was made for man, man was not made for Sabbath," even the Sabbath Day, which is a day of rest and of worshipping Him.

Our political parties are good and were given to us by God, but we have begun worshipping the gift, not the giver of the gift. He does not want us to discontinue the use of our parties, but He does want us to give Him praise and thanks for giving us the gift. As a nation, when was the last time we dedicated a time to stop and say "We praise you, Lord, because you are God and we thank you for the gifts"? because the Bible says "All good and perfect gifts come from above."

But at this time, 2001, God wants Pat Robertson to be president and Rev. Jesse Jackson to be vice president for two reasons. The first because we as a nation have become wayward (a harlot) and we need to repent and show our Father in heaven that we honor Him and these two men who represent Him. The second reason is that we as a nation need these two men. They are both men of God, ministers of the Gospel, preachers. We need Jesse Jackson because he knows the ways of the world. Whenever there are problems in other nations, he is one of first to come to mind (if not the very first) and has been chosen to go to other nations to assist in matters.

We need the Rev. Pat Robertson because he knows the future of the world. Our nation and all others are embarking upon times in this world that are considered end times, or the Last Days. Pat Robertson operates in the Gifts of the Spirit, which are spoken of in the fourteenth chapter of the book of First Corinthians, and is also a student and teacher of eschatology (end times or the last days).

Allow me to pause to clarify the two terms that I used earlier in this subject: "God's permissive will and His perfect will." His permissive will is the ventures that ungodly people (and something godly as well) seek to do on their own, because they do not know the will of God, which is written in His Word, and He actually allows those things to be, only to show men many times that, that is not what they needed or that He had a much better plan for mankind, according to His Word. God used King David to help His people. He used King Hezekiah to lead His people back to Him. I believe it is

God's perfect will to use Rev. Pat Robertson and Rev. Jesse Jackson to lead His people back to Him and deliver them from their problems in this nation.

God's perfect will can be defined by and/or seen in the nation of Israel or the United States when really needing someone to rescue them when they are unable to rescue or deliver themselves.

When the ten northern tribes of Israel were taken into captivity by Assyria, twenty years later King Sennacherib of Assyria came to Jerusalem to take King Hezekiah, the capital city, Jerusalem, and all of Judah into captivity. These are the words of Sennacherib, king of Assyria, that can be found in 2 Kings 18:31 (NLT):

> "Don't listen to Hezekiah when he tries to mislead you by saying, 'The Lord will rescue us!' Have the gods of any other nations ever saved their people from the King of Assyria? What happened to the gods of Hamath and Arpad? And what about the gods of Sepharvaim, Hena, and Ivvah? Did they rescue Samaria from my power? What god of any nation has ever been able to save its people from my power? Name just one! So what makes you think that the Lord can rescue Jerusalem?"

> But the people were silent and did not answer because Hezekiah had told them not to speak. Then Eliakim son of Hilkiah, the palace administrator, Shebna the court secretary, and Joah son of Asaph, the royal historian, went back to Hezekiah. They tore their clothes in despair (as a sign of humility before God) and they went in to see the King and told him what the Assyrian representative had said.

When King Hezekiah heard their report, he tore his
clothes and put on sackcloth and went into the Temple
of the Lord to pray. (2 Kings 19:1)

Can you imagine a king taking off his royal robe to put on
sackcloth or tearing his clothes just to humble himself before his
Holy God? He is the same Holy God that we in America serve today.

And he sent Eliakim the palace administrator, Shebna
the court secretary, and the leading priest, all dressed
in sackcloth, to the prophet Isaiah son of Amoz. They
told him, "This is what King Hezekiah says: This is
a day of trouble, insult, and disgrace. It is like when
a child is ready to be born, but the mother has no
strength to deliver it. But perhaps the Lord your God
has heard the Assyrian representative defying the
living God and will punish him for his words. Oh
pray for those of us who are left." (v 2)

After King Hezekiah's officials delivered the king's message to
Isaiah, the prophet replied, "Say to your master. This is what the
Lord says: Do not be disturbed by this blasphemous speech against
me from the Assyrian king's messengers. Listen! I myself will move
against him, and the king will receive a report from Assyria telling
him that he is needed at home. Then I will make him want to return
to his land, where I will have him killed with a sword."

Meanwhile, the Assyrian representative left Jerusalem and went
to consult his king, who had left Lachish and was attacking Libnah.
Soon afterward, King Sennacherib received word that King Tirhakah
of Ethiopia was leading an army to fight against him. Before leaving to
meet the attack, he sent this message back to Hezekiah in Jerusalem:

This message is for King Hezekiah of Judah. Don't let this God you trust deceive you with promises that Jerusalem will not be captured by the King of Assyria.

You know perfectly well what the Kings of Assyria have done wherever they have gone. They have crushed everyone who stood in their way! Why should you be any different? Have the gods of other nations rescued them—such nations as Gozan, Haran, Rezeph, and the people of Eden who were in Tel-assar? The former kings of Assyria destroyed them all! What happened to the King of Hamath and the King of Aspad? What happened to the Kings of Sepharvaim, Hena, and Ivvah?

After Hezekiah received the letter and read it, he went up to the Lord's Temple and spread it out before the Lord. And Hezekiah prayed this prayer before the Lord: O Lord, God of Israel, you are enthroned between the mighty cherubim! You alone are God of all the kingdoms of the earth. You alone created the heavens and the earth. Listen to me, O Lord, and hear! Open your eyes, O Lord, and see! Listen to Sennacherib's words of defiance against the living God.

It is true, Lord, that the Kings of Assyria have destroyed all these nations, just as the message says. And they have thrown the gods of these nations into the fire and burn them. But of course the Assyrians could destroy them! They were not gods at all—only idols of wood and stone shaped by human hands. Now, O Lord our God, rescue us from his power; then all the kingdoms of the earth will know that You alone O Lord, are God.

Then Isaiah son of Amoz sent this message to Hezekiah:

This is what the Lord, the God of Israel, says: I
have heard your prayer about King Sennacherib of
Assyria. This is the message that the Lord has spoken
against Him:

The virgin daughter of Zion
despises you and laughs at you
The daughter of Jerusalem
scoffs and shakes her head as you flee
Whom do you think you have
been insulting and ridiculing?
Against whom did you raise
your voice?
At whom did you look in such
proud condescension?
It was the Holy One of Israel!
By your messengers you have
mocked the Lord.
You have said, "With my many chariots.
I have conquered the highest mountains—
Yes, the remotest peaks of Lebanon
I have cut down its tallest cedars
and its choicest cypress trees.
I have reached its farthest corners
and explored its deepest forests.
I have dug wells in many a foreign land
and refreshed myself with their water.
I even stopped up the rivers of Egypt
so that my armies could go across!"
"But have you not heard?

It was I, the Lord, who decided this long ago.

Long ago I planned what I am now causing to happen,

that you should crush fortified cities into heaps of rubble.

That is why their people have so little power

and are such easy prey for you.

They are as helpless as the grass,

as easily trampled as tender green shoots.

They are like grass sprouting

on a housetop,

But I know you well—

your comings and goings and all you do.

I know the way you have raged against me.

And because of your arrogance against me,

which I have heard for myself,

I will put My bridle in your mouth,

I will make you return

by the road on which you came."

Then Isaiah said to Hezekiah,

Here is the proof that the Lord will protect this city from Assyria's king. This year you will eat only what grows up by itself, and next year you will eat what springs up from that. But in the third year you will tend vineyards and eat their fruit. And you who are left in Judah, who have escaped the ravages of the siege, will take root again in your own soil, and you will flourish and multiply. For a remnant of My people will spread out from Jerusalem, a group of survivors from Mount Zion. The passion (zeal) of the Lord Almighty will make this happen!

And this is what the Lord says about the king of Assyria:

> His armies will not enter Jerusalem to shoot their
> arrows. They will not march outside its gates with
> their shields and build banks of earth against its walls.
> The king will return to his own county by the road
> on which he came. He will not enter the city, says
> the Lord. For My own honor and for the sake of My
> servant David, I will defend it.

That night the angel of the Lord went out to the Assyrian camp and killed 185,000 Assyrian troops. When the surviving Assyrian woke up the next morning, they found corpses everywhere. Then King Sennacherib of Assyria broke camp and returned to his own land. He went home to his capital of Nineveh and stayed there. One day while he was worshiping in the temple of his god Nisrock, his sons Adrammeelech and Sharezer killed him with their swords. They then escaped to the land of Ararat, and another son, Esarhaddon, became the next king of Assyria.

As we study our Bibles and see what God did to bring other nations against His chosen people, Israel, and as He brought judgment against other nations such as Assyria because of arrogance, please know that He is also dealing with our nation and bringing judgment against us. We are reaping what we have sown. We took prayer out of our schools in 1962, and forty years later we had to deal with what happened at Columbine High. Because of what the FBI did at Ruby Ridge and Branch Davidian and especially what J. Edger Hoover did leading the FBI, causing the death of one of America's greatest presidents, President John F. Kennedy, we had to deal with the Oklahoma Bombing. Because of our national leaders taking prayer, Bible reading, and all godliness out of all public settings, we had to deal with an attack on the Pentagon. And lastly, because of what some think (even in our own nation) that New York City is Mystery Babylon spoken of in Revelation 18:9–11, we had to deal with what happened to the Twin Trade Towers.

Hear what Dr. Noah Hutchings and Southwest Radio Church Ministries' October 2001 *Prophetic Observer* had to say:

> I have been to Babylon on the Euphrates as restored by Saddam Hussein. This Babylon we know. It is no mystery. It cannot be the "Mystery Babylon" of Revelation 18. The Babylon of Revelation is the greatest commercial city that exists in the last days. In world importance, it is comparable to the Babylon of Nebuchadnezzar's day. Of Mystery Babylon of the end time, we read:
>
> "And the kings of the earth, who have committed fornication and lived deliciously with her, shall bewail her and lament for her, when they shall see smoke of her burning. Standing afar off for the fear of her torment, saying Alas, alas that city Babylon that mighty city! For in one hour is thy judgment come. And the merchants of the earth shall weep and mourn over her, for no man buyeth their merchandise any more." (Rev. 18:9–11)
>
> It grieves my soul to even make a comparison between Revelation 18 and what happened to New York City on September 11, 2001. Nevertheless, the similarities are striking. New York City is the greatest commercial port city in the world. It is traditionally called "The

Babylon on the Hudson." Across the bay is Babylon, New York, part of the metro complex. The fall of the Twin Trade Towers, symbols of world commerce, fell within one hour, and on television we saw thousands upon thousands around the world joining in mourning this awful tragedy. Many prophecies in the Bible are conditional, like Jonah's declaration, "Forty days and Nineveh will be destroyed." 'Nineveh repented, and the city was spared, New York City, or the entire nation, does not have to be Mystery Babylon. "Please repent; national leaders, media, and all that are involved in the world commerce of New York City."

The writer closes by stating,

It is true we have forsaken God in many ways. We no longer allow our children to pray and read the Bible in public schools. We have allowed the killing of the unborn. Few of our churches now worship the Lord Jesus Christ as both Savior and Creator of all things in heaven and on earth. We have become a sinful and wicked nation. But our time for repenting before God and seeking His forgiveness is short.

A Turning Point?

Also from October, 2001 issue of the *Prophetic Observer* (last page):

I was disturbed because the Name of Jesus Christ was not mentioned or honored more in the prayer and ceremonies after the Manhattan tragedy. However, our president did seek help from God out of the Scriptures. Many in Congress did attend a prayer service in the Capital Rotunda. Churches and individual Christians across the nation were called upon to pray and seek God's help and comfort, and it was so good to hear our people once again stand up and declare that it was good to be an American. Just maybe God will hear us as a nation, seeking His forgiveness, and help. If so, then those who died at the World Trade Towers and the Pentagon, as well as those innocent souls on the airplanes, will not have died in vain.

In the beginning sentence of this writing, the writer makes a very serious observation. I noticed it myself during the service: The Name of Jesus Christ was not mentioned or honored during the prayer and ceremonies after the Manhattan tragedy. "Children of America," the Bible says "if His Name is lifted up (or highly honored), God would draw all men unto Himself," and they would receive an eternal blessing. The Bible says, "There is no other Name under heaven given by which men may be saved, it is the only way we can be saved; our faith in Christ." The Bible also says "that at the Name of Jesus Christ every knee will bow and every tongue will confess that He is Lord to the glory of God our Father." As a child growing up among six cousins, the Moores and a younger brother Hue, living with our grandmother, she would tell us horror stories from the book of Revelation. "In the last days," she would say, "when the Lord comes, men will hide behind large rocks. The rocks will skip away and say, 'Don't hide behind us, it is too late.'"

Repent while there is time, America. Confess and make Him (Christ) your Lord while there is still time.

America needs to pray for the lesbian and feminist agenda. In the sixties there was a very popular song entitled "I am woman." The words to that song were "I am woman, here me roar." It was a time of great liberties. There was free love, free sex, and it seemed the entire nation was adjusting to blacks obtaining their free rights regarding equal employment and women gaining their equal rights because of their gender. America's history tells us that at the turn of the twentieth century, in the early 1900s, men were allowed to spank their wives as if they were little children. In the sixties women began having barn fire (as it were) in the middle of the streets of major cities, burning their bras. Shouting (as it were) "I am woman, hear me roar," "give me my equal rights." From that,

November 16, 2001

A feminist movement, it seems, began. In 1969, shortly after I began my employment at Texas Instruments, I noticed a white young lady who was assisting in a job assignment. She had purchased a brand-new MG Midget sports car. She wore jeans all the time, and she always walked holding her shoulders up as if she was attempting to walk like a man. I did notice the way she carried herself, but I did not give too much thought to it. It was in the late seventies when I began watching women tennis. Billie Jean King was the American champion, and I noticed her hair was cut short like Pat's, the young lady that I worked with in 1969, and she walked and carried herself in a similar way. I still did not give that much thought.

Later, on national television, she came out. Her girlfriend was suing her. It became clear what was going on in our nation. Growing up in Temple, Texas, as young folk we would always hear of this one man walking around the Eight Street area, which was the popular place for us young folk because of A-1 Drive Inn. It was a Dairy Queen for Blacks. I was a teenager, and I sometimes saw that gentleman walking along. As a young person, you sometimes will not allow yourself to think certain things. I could see the way the gentleman carried himself, but I would not allow myself to consider why he did. It was the same with Pat and Ms. King.

I'd like to take this time to thank God for Billie Jean King because she made women tennis what it is today. And if anyone in this nation wanted to gain information regarding lesbians and the feminist agenda, I believe she would be the person that I would look to. I believe she is a woman of integrity. I believe Ellen DeGeneres is a very special lady also, but it seems she is in the thick of things going on in this nation, and that could cause much pressure in her life. God has also put Martina in my heart. I wish each of these ladies well.

Regarding this feminist movement, it has been said that Ms. Hillary Clinton was homosexual and also leading in this movement. I prayed for Ms. Clinton to obtain the position of the senator for New York. I have sinned greatly in my life before becoming a Christian. And as Christians we still have weaknesses. Homosexuality is a sin like all other sins. The Bible does say that it is an abomination unto God, which means it is the worst kind, the most hideous, but there is no sin that God cannot forgive and also deliver an individual from.

Regarding my prayer for Ms. Clinton, I prayed because I thought she would be representing the people and more issues that I thought would be more godly. I also prayed for former President Clinton to be made president because of a testimony he gave regarding his state of Arkansas helping the underprivileged and those on welfare. From what he said, I also thought he would glorify the Lord Jesus Christ more. During the full eight years of him being in office, Christ our Lord was never mentioned that I know of. It seems it is the same way with Ms. Clinton. In these last days, God is our only source of help, and His Word says all we do should be done by faith in His Son and in Christ Jesus's name.

Again, regarding this feminist movement, it seems as if the female homosexuals are working to support not only gay rights but also women to be put in power. As mentioned before, these ladies are cutting their hair short and, it seems, also creating a fad. In time past most women wore their hair long or up, but never cut. The Bible says a woman's hair is her glory, meaning it is something she can be really proud of, that God has blessed her with it.

January 6, 2002

Women of America, and other nations of the world, please know that God loves you deeply. His Word declares it. You are not second-class people. But as women He expects more of you. Please hear what the apostle Paul says to the Roman church and you:

> But God shows His anger from heaven against all sinful, wicked people who push the truth away from themselves. For the truth about God is known to them instinctively. God has put this knowledge in their hearts. From the time the world was created, people have seen the earth and sky and all that God made. They can clearly see His invisible qualities— His eternal power and divine nature. So they have no excuse whatsoever for not knowing God. (Rom. 1:18–2:11 NLT)

Yes, they knew God, but they wouldn't worship him as God or even give Him thanks. And they began to think up foolish ideas of what God was like. The result was that their minds became dark and confused. Claiming to be wise, they became utter fools instead. And instead of worshiping the glorious, ever-living God, they worshipped idols made to look like mere people, or birds and animals and snakes.

So God let them go ahead and do whatever shameful things their hearts desired. As a result, they did vile and degrading things with each other's bodies. Instead of believing what they knew was the truth about God, they deliberately chose to believe lies. So they worshipped the things God made, not the Creator Himself, who is to be praised forever. Amen.

That is why God abandoned them to their shameful desires. Even the women turned against the natural way to have sex and instead indulged in sex with each other. And the men, instead of having normal sexual relationship with women, burned with lust for each other. Men did shameful things with other men and, as a result, suffered within themselves the penalty they so richly deserved.

When they refused to acknowledge God, he abandoned them to their evil minds and let them do things that should never be done. Their lives became full of every kind of wickedness, sin, greed, hate, envy, murder, fighting, deception, malicious behavior, and gossip. They are backbiters, haters of God, insolent, proud, and boastful. They are forever inventing new ways of sinning and are disobedient to their parents. They refuse to understand, break their promises, and are heartless and unforgiving. They are fully aware of God's death penalty for those who do these things, yet they go right ahead and do them anyway. And worse yet, they encourage others to do them too.

You may be saying, "What terrible people you have been speaking of!" But you are just as bad, and you have no excuse! When you say they are wicked and should be punished, you are condemning yourself, for you do these very same things. And we know that God, in his justice, will punish anyone who does such things. Do you think that God will judge and condemn others for doing them and not judge you when you do them too? Don't you realize how kind, tolerant, and patient God is with you? Or don't you care? Can't you see how kind He has been in giving you time to turn from your sin?

But no, you won't listen. So you are storing up terrible punishment for yourself because of your stubbornness in refusing to turn from your sin. For there is going to come a day of judgment when God, the just judge of all the world will judge all people according to what they have done. He will give eternal life to those who persist in doing what is good, seeking after the glory and honor and immortality that God offers. But He will pour out His anger and wrath on those who live for themselves, who refuse to obey the truth and practice evil deeds. There will be trouble and calamity for everyone who keeps on sinning, for the Jew first and also for the Gentile. But there will be glory and honor and peace from God for all who do good, for the Jew first and also for the Gentile. For God does not show favoritism.

Concerning our women and the divorce rate, the Bible says women are made to be a helpmeet (mate) for their husband. It is why the divorce rate is more than 50 percent in America. Women, when you are working on your jobs establishing a career, consider the strain that is being put on your marriage. God said you were to be a helpmeet for your husband. You are fighting against yourselves because you are a part of that marriage, and when you go to work, you cannot devote yourself to your marriage, which you are a part of. You are working on something that has nothing to do with your marriage. Thus, you're putting a great strain on that marriage, and more than 50 percent of the time we have a divorce because of it, "said God!" The Bible says your life should be toward your husband. Remember, God wants you to be a helpmeet for your husband.

There are many men that want their wives to work so that the income can be supplemented. But whether he wants her to work or not, God said that she is—that is, her entire life is to be toward (devoted to) her husband or to be there for that marriage. It is a holy marriage set by God, and no other way will work in our lives except the way that He has set these things in order for our lives.

Again, consider our divorce rate in this nation. We are a disgrace to God and to all other nations because of our divorce rate, "said God!" If things are going on in the husband's life that demands encouraging, comforting, and/or strengthening, the wife should be there for him. How can she be there for him if she has her own career and agenda established and is on her job when he needs some help or someone to talk to. If she tries to comfort him while she is at work, then she is cheating her employer and will eventually get fired. We need to do it God's way—consider the divorce rate. Also consider God Almighty made you two one, not two separate individuals to do your own separate things. But in these last days, He is going to show us that He means what He says in His Word.

January 2002

Regarding families supplementing their income, I have two businesses, both of which are multilevel marketing that usually takes no more than two to four hours per day per business. In my AMWAY business, there in my up line (the person that bought into this business before I purchased it) is a gentleman, Louie Curillo, that lost his job as an air traffic controller. After almost losing his home and everything he owned, he finally landed a position in a detective agency. During the time that he did, his wife, Kathy, was invited to an AMWAY meeting. She invited him to go with her. He refused flatly, saying "no way."

She continued to attend the meetings and did purchase the business. She continued to ask him to the meetings. He continued to say "Absolutely not." His position in the agency was elevating, but after her being persistent about getting him to one of the meetings to see how great the results were in the lives of others people, he decided to accompany her to a meeting. After hearing the great things said about this business, he considered it, but his position as a detective continued to be elevated. She continued to work the business.

Finally, after seeing how determined she was regarding making this business work, he decided to join her, but his position as a detective was still going up. He began working the business after he got home from his regular job each evening. With a secured salary of $70,000 annually and offer to become a partner in the agency, he decided to go with AMWAY. Now they make hundreds of thousands of dollars yearly, but without his wife working the business when he was on his regular job, they would never have been as successful as they are.

For couples that want their income supplemented, wives can work this business a few hours per day, set her schedule any way she likes, and more importantly be there for her husband and children, if there are children in your lives.

When God created the heavens and the earth, He was only concerned about man and his family. He said to man, "Be fruitful, and multiply, and replenish the earth, and subdue it" (take complete control over all creatures) "and have dominion over the fish of the sea, and over the fowl of the air and over every living thing that moveth upon the earth" (Gen 1:28). "And God said, Behold, I have given you every herb bearing seed, which is upon the face of all the earth and every tree, in the which is the fruit of a tree yielding seed; to you it shall be for meat" (v 29). "And to every beast of the earth, and to every fowl of the air, and to every thing that creepeth upon the earth, wherein there is life, I have given every green herb for meat; and it was so" (v 30).

God has given man everything in the earth for him and his family. Genesis 2:7 says, "And the Lord God formed man of the earth of the dust of the ground, and breathed into his nostrils the breath of life, and man became a living soul." "And out of the ground the Lord God formed every beast of the field, and every fowl of the air, and brought them unto Adam to see what he would call them: and whatsoever Adam called every living creature, that was the name thereof" (v 19). "And Adam gave names to all cattle, and to the fowl of the air, and to every beast of the field; but for Adam there was not found an helpmeet for him" (v 20).

At this time in the earth Eve had not been created, but after Adam named the animals, "the Lord God caused a deep sleep to fall upon Adam, and he slept: and He took one of his ribs, and closed up the flesh instead thereof" (v 21) "and the rib", which the Lord God had taken from man, made he a woman, and brought her unto the man. God made woman for man to be a helpmeet for him; not only did He make her for him; He (God) made her from him, and also presented her to him (v 22).

God created all living things and gave them to man. When He created Eve, all things became theirs, and when they had children, all things became the entire family and were eventually passed to the children as an inheritance.

> Where is the man who fears the Lord? God will teach him how to choose the best. He shall live with God's circle of blessing, and his children shall inherit the earth. (Ps. 25:12–13)

FAMILY NEWS FROM DR. JAMES DOBSON

At this late date as I am about to issue this letter (book) to Dr. Hutchings, not having the time to write in longhand as I have this entire book. I do not want to take any more time in delaying this material, so please accept this newsletter from Dr. James Dobson regarding Father and Son. It is very needed information for the fathers of America. I am a father and grandfather. I cannot stress enough the need for Psalms 78, the first eight verses regarding "teaching the wonders of God to our children" (v 4). "We will not hide them from their children, showing to the generation to come the praises of the Lord, and His strength, and His wonderful works that He hath done."

Also Proverbs 22:6, "Train up a child in the way he should go: and when he is old, he will not depart from it," should be important in the lives of all American parents.

Parents, please consider, meditate and pray for God's guidance regarding how you may apply this information in your lives.

January 2002

We are in trouble, America! The president says he believes in God. He needs to come before our nation and declare to the people he is not going to continue on as he has. He should let the people know how much trouble we are really in and also let the leaders and the American people know, in all humility, that he cannot and will not continue on like this. "We need God's help," he should declare. "Look at our divorce rate, look at the violence in our nation, and promiscuity (including teenage pregnancy) and many other statistics that show we have gotten ourselves in trouble and only a God (if He will) will deliver us. I declare I'm going to seek his help, and if the other leaders of this nation choose not to follow me, I believe our founders, especially Abraham Lincoln, would say 'I will step down,' for I cannot and will not try to lead this nation without God's help and I will not keep my faith in a closet. The scriptures declare, 'If we deny Him before men, He (the Lord Jesus Christ) will deny us before His Heavenly Father and angels.'"

If our president were to step down because of ungodly leaders deciding not to follow him, God Almighty would still bless him, for he would then have all the eyes of the whole earth on him, watching him seek his God. Remember Martin Luther King Jr.! We need God's help, America!

If our president did step down and the vice president became president, I personally believe God would deal with him severely if he did not seek God's help because his generation is the one that took God out of all public settings, starting with our schools.

January 20, 2002

I thank God for all the work that is being done by celebrities, especially the entertainers (those in film, music, comedy, and sports), but the media talk show hosts and politicians as well.

The Lord Jesus Christ admonished (encouraged) a religious person when he asked, "What is the first commandment." Answering, Jesus said, "To love God with all your heart, soul, mind, and strength, and the second is like unto it, to love your neighbor as your self." The religious person said, "Thou hast well said." Jesus perceived man's understanding and said, "You're not far from the kingdom of God." Allow me to say, all of you celebrities that are reaching out to help hurting humanity by founding or supporting nonprofit organizations, you're not far from the Kingdom of God.

Matthew 25:34–40 (KJV),

> Then shall the King say unto them on his right hand,
> Come, ye blessed of my Father (God Almighty) inherit
> the kingdom prepared for you from the foundation of
> the world.
>
> For I was hungry, and ye gave me meat: I was thirsty
> and ye gave me drink: I was a stranger, and ye took
> me in.

Naked, and ye clothed me: I was sick, and ye visited me: I was in prison and ye came unto me.

Then shall the righteous answer Him, saying, Lord, when saw we thee an hungred, and fed thee? or thirsty, and gave thee a drink?

When saw we thee a stranger, and took thee in? or naked, and clothed thee?

Or when saw we sick or in prison, and came unto thee?

And the King shall answer and say unto them, verily I say unto you, Inasmuch as ye have done it unto the least of these my brethren, ye have done it unto me.

Please know, celebrity people, that you are in the thoughts and in the heart of the Lord Jesus Christ, because of the great things you are doing to help hurting people. More important than you being on His heart and in His thoughts is Him wanting to be in your heart. The only way that can happen is you inviting Him into your heart and asking Him to forgive you of sin. He loves you! Do you believe it?

As I consider all the work that celebrities are doing to help God's people, such as Reagan Hughes, the former Miss Texas and Miss America first runner up, volunteering time to support Big Brothers and Big Sisters, nonprofit group, which is one of my favorite because as a child growing up in the house of my grandmother, Celester Dotsey, with my younger brother Hue Barrett, I did not have an older (or "big") brother. Also living with my grandmother were my cousins, the Moores, Robert and his brothers and sisters, Treva, Mary, Billy (who was my age, two months older), Liz, and Anthony.

Not having a big brother bothered me so much I adopted Robert as my big brother. He was the oldest of eight grandchildren. The younger children would at times want to follow Robert any place he went, especially me. Because he was the eldest, our grandmother would allow him to go to Mr. J. K. Wilkerson soda and Malt shop. His younger siblings wanted to follow (or tag along), but myself even more as if he were my big brother. All the grandchildren living with my grandmother were members of Progressive Baptist Church in Cameron, Texas, including Robert. But when he became a teen, he met a young girl, Charlie Mae, and wanted to join the Church of Christ that she was a member of in our community. Our grandmother trusted him and all of her grandchildren. None of us were ever involved in problems at school, with the law, in our community, or any place else. She was very strict, and we loved and respected her for it. Because she did trust Robert, she allowed him to join the Church of Christ. All of his brothers and sisters continued at Progressive Baptist, but I followed Robert to the Church of Christ. After a while, I rejoined the others at Progressive, but I like being around my adopted big brother.

When Robert graduated high school, he was drafted into the military (the Army). It was a time of war in Vietnam when warfare was very severe, during 1967 to 1968. When he returned home, he told us war stories you wouldn't believe. One attack on his troop left his best friend holding his intestines in his hands when a hand grenade exploded. There were many young men that lost their lives that we knew there in the small town of Cameron. We thanked God for bringing our big brother home safely.

I also thank God for Reagan Hughes of Dallas/Mesquite, Texas, joining Big Brothers and Big Sisters Mentoring Organization. Also, Robert Flores and Pete Kenworthy of KWTX, Chanel 10, both Sports Persons in Waco, Texas, supporting the Waco Branch.

Oprah Winfrey has founded the Angel Network Non-Profit Group, and many other celebrities have either joined an existing nonprofit group or have founded one in their own name such as the Whitney Houston Foundation, the Paula McClure Cancer Foundation for Women, the William "Bill" Cosby Foundation, the Todd Bridges Foundation, the Tom Joyner Foundation, the Tiger Woods Foundation, the Mike Madono Foundation, the Troy Aikman Foundation, and the Dallas Maverick Foundation—all of which I believe is a result of prayer. Men of the Cloth, please do not be upset with me because of the title of this book, "The Book Two." I want and my prayer is this book will live forever because of all the people names listed in this book that have great things to help God's people. God's Word says He is not respector of person. As He has bkessed the names of many in the Bible (The Book One – the Book above all books), He will also bless people of our generation, because He is no respector of persons, says the Word of God.

Again, as the Lord Jesus Christ commended the religious leader in his faith in God by telling him "You, sir, are not far from the Kingdom," allow me to say Christ Jesus is watching every good work you are doing and great effort you are making. Again, He said, "When you've done these things to the least of my brethren, you done them unto Me," and I say I believe He would have me to say, because all of your good works, you are not far from the Kingdom of God. He is watching and waiting with open arms, saying "I stand at the door (of your heart) and knock. If you will invite me in, I will come in and sup with you and you with Me." Please hear His voice and know that He is waiting, and He knows every good work you've done.

I also thank God for the large number of celebrities giving great effort to these organizations, such as Sara Michelle Gellar giving her summer vacation time of relaxation and enjoyment up to help Habitat Homes for Humanity during the late nineties, Lou Rawls supporting Negro College Funds for many years, Jerry Lewis supporting Jerry Kid for many years, as well as Marlow Thomas for St. Jude, Mary Tyler Moore for Juvenile Diabetes.

In Dallas, Texas, alone there is Jane McGary supporting the Dare to Care Organization, Clarice Tinsley supporting the Metropley Mentoring Organization, and she was a longtime supporter of the Juvenile Diabetes Foundation before assisting the Metropley Mentoring Org. There is Dale Henson supporting Dallas and Fort Worth Can Academy. Also, there is Paula McClure Founding a Cancer Organization for Women. God is going to bless each of you and others that were not named. My prayer is that you allow Him to bless you spiritually by inviting Christ Jesus into your hearts.

I believe many of you have founded an organization or are supporting other nonprofit groups because of the prayer of the saints, especially my prayers for you daily.

Britney Spears, God is watching over you. Todd Bridges and Tonyo Harding, God wants to bless you and see you back on top. Give Him thanks!

Todd Bridges the Lord will not let me forget how effective you, Gary Coleman, and Dana Plato were in touching our nation through the weekly TV show "Different Strokes." A show that allowed us to see a white man and his daughter, played by Dana Pato, bring two young black boys, Willis played by you and Arnold, his little brother, Gary Coleman. God will not let me forget how effective you were as an older brother when Willis would not let his white stepdad spank his younger brother. Willis said, "I don't think you have a right to spank my little brother, I should do it." Mr. Drummin, the stepdad, agreed and allowed this little twelve or thirteen-year-old to discipline his younger brother. The most interesting part of that episode was that Arnold thought his big brother had gotten him off the hook and that he would not be spanked. When Willis took him to the bedroom to spank him, Arnold asked, "What are you going hit to make it sound like my butt?" Willis's reply was "Your butt."

It showed great integrity, and when you got yourself in trouble in real life, it may have seemed that you let many people down. But you cannot let God down or make Him displeased when He knows our every weakness and He wants to raise you up again. We all know the Bible story of David and Goliath. David was a young boy when he killed that giant. When he became a man, God made him the greatest king this world has ever seen. As a king he saw Bathsheba bathing on the roof of her house where it was cool and private. David happened to see her while bathing. He sent for her, slept with her, and got her pregnant. He first tried to cover up his sin, but that didn't work, so he had her husband put on the front line in battle to be killed. God killed that baby because it was conceived the wrong way.

In Psalm 51, David repented, asked God to forgive him. God did forgive him and gave him another baby, and that one grew up, and God made him the second greatest king that has ever lived. His name was Solomon and was the wisest man that had ever lived.

The only man greater and wiser is the Lord Jesus Christ. He confirmed it when He said "Greater than Solomon has come."

God made David a promise that "one is coming that will sit on your throne forever." Even until this day the Lord Jesus Christ is called "the Son of David." God does not forget His promises. All He wants us to do is to ask Him to forgive us of sin and to "reach out" and help our fellow man.

Know that God is with you, Tonya Harding, Joyce Dewitt, O. J. Simpson, and others that may be spoken of in a negative way. He loves you. Do you believe it?

My son Terrence's life was affected because of you, Todd and Gary Coleman. At the age of eight years old he came to me and said, "Daddy, I want to be like Arnold on 'Different Strokes.'" At approximately twelve he appeared in back-to-school fashion for Dillard's in Dallas. At sixteen he made his first commercial for Lewisville Police, north of Dallas, and appeared as stand-in for a movie that John Ritter starred in, another movie that Chuck Norris starred in. Other jobs as well. All because of Arnold, or Gary Coleman and Willis on "Different Strokes." When Terrence was growing up, I would tell him God's promises that are in the Bible and that they are for us. And then I would ask him, "Do you believe it?" His reply would always be yes.

Celebrity people! God loves you! Do you believe it?

Again, I pray for celebrities daily, many times calling them by name. Those that are in politics, the media, talk show hosts. But especially entertainment (film, music, comedy, and sports). I am doing all that I can to watch over God's people in prayer. All people in this nation and other parts of the earth.

March 31, 2002
Easter Sunday

Saturday, March 23, I purposely prayed for Halle Berry to win the Oscar (which was given on the following day, the Lord's Day). I prayed that day because I did not want to go in prayer on the Lord's Day, speaking about all the great things going on in the world. We know Satan is the god of this world system.

The reason I prayed for her to win the Oscar is because in prayer, ten years ago, I told the Lord "We need to come together in this nation," even in intermarriage. And because black men for a very long time marrying white women may have offended white men. So by faith in Christ I lifted up our women in prayer—that is, black women—and asked God to bless their relationship with white men so that black men would no longer be an offense to their white brothers.

After that prayer, white men began dating and marrying blacks. One couple here in Temple had recently moved to town. They visited our church, Victory Baptist. After that, movies were made with white men and black women coming together, such as *The Eraser* with Arnold Schwarzenegger and Vanessa Williams and other sitcoms and weekly TV shows. Children of America (both young and old), we do not have the right to offend each other, and if black men dating and marrying white women offend our white brothers, we need to release in our hearts the right for our white brothers to date and marry black women if they want.

The movie that landed Ms. Berry an Oscar nomination was *Monster's Ball*. A movie where a black lady allowed herself to become involved with a white man whose father hated blacks with a passion. I've not seen the movie, but we're told "it is worthy of an Oscar," and she did win. The reason that I haven't seen the movie is, I do not go to the movie anymore to see secular shows. The last movie I saw at the movies was *Black Stallion* with Terrence when he was twelve years old. He's now thirty. Except two years back where Paul and Matthew Crouch asked all Christians to watch the movie *The Omega Code*. There is a part 2. We encourage you to see both movies (regarding the end of the world).

A few weeks before praying for my daughter, Ms. Berry, I refer to her as my daughter because I pray for her so much (as if she is), an advertising with Denzel Washington appearing in a movie, depicting a father whose son was about to die as he lay in the hospital. Again, I've not seen the movie, but I did see a frantic mother look at her desperate husband and say "Do something." She represented every woman in this nation. She submitted herself to her husband as the authority of their family as she should according to God's Word and allowed that burden to rest on him.

For over two hundred years white women have conducted themselves in a very gentle and submissive way. To say that I thank God for that spirit being in them would be an understatement. And here we have this little black lady conducting herself in the same way, means that the movie should win an Oscar simply because of what she did.

In the advertisement, we see Mr. Washington, from great desperation, began to hold individuals hostage. When his wife looked at him in great despair and said "Do something," God allowed that burden to rest on me as if what was going on in that movie was real. To be honest I did not know what to do.

Men of America, we should not allow our women to bear heavy burdens on themselves. We should be there for them. And please believe me when I say we do not have what it takes to carry those cares ourselves. As I considered what I should do if I were faced with this problem, fright tried to capture my heart, and my God allowed me to carry that burden for your sake, America, so that I could later tell you what His Word says.

When Hosea, the prophet, was instructed by God to marry Gomer, a prostitute, it was done so that Hosea could feel what God felt toward the nation of Israel because she prostituted herself by serving other gods.

God wants me to tell you, men of America and the world, we do not have the strength, wisdom, or knowledge to bear or carry burdens of this life.

As I considered what was happening in that movie with that father carrying that burden, God allowed me to feel the burden of every woman bringing their cares to men. Men, that is what they should do. The question is, What are you going to do with those burdens?

After the Lord allowed me to carry that burden for about two weeks, He reminded me what His Word says: "Cast your cares upon me because I care for you." Then He reminded me of the story of Jacob and Rachel when she (Rachel) could not bear any children because God had shut up her womb.

Rachel said unto Jacob, "Give me children, or else I die" (KJV).

Men, she did what she should. She went to her husband. Jacob's reply was, "Am I in God's stead, who hath withheld from thee the fruit of the womb?" (KJV).

The New Living Version says, "Am I God? He is the only one able to give you children."

First of all, men, we're not God. That is why Jacobs reply was "Am I God?"

As I considered all the burdens of women that brought them to their husbands, fear did try to grip my heart. It was as if every person in this nation and others throughout the earth was looking at me as they said to themselves, "Let's see what this idiot is going to do." My reply, as should yours be, brothers, is "Am I God?" Brothers, we do not have what it takes to carry those burdens, nor should we want to.

Jacob told his wife, "God is the only one able to give you children." Men, God is the only one able to carry your burden.

In Matthew 11:28–30, Jesus speaking says,

> Come unto Me, all ye that labour (work hard at trying to resolve all of your issues in life) and are heavy laden (burdened), and I will give you rest.

> Take My yoke upon you, and learn of Me; for I am meek and lowly in heart: and ye shall find rest unto your souls.

> For My yoke is easy, and my burden is light. (KJV)

The New Living Translation says,

> Come to Me, all of you who are weary and carry heavy burdens, and I will give you rest. Take My yoke upon

you. Let me teach you, because I am humble and
gentle, and you will find rest for your souls. For My
yoke fits perfectly, and the burden I give you is light.

Brothers, cast your cares upon the Lord. He loves you, and He is
the only one able to carry your burdens. Please bow your knees and
your hearts to the Lord Jesus Christ and say, "Dear God, forgive my
sin and help me to cast this care (burden) and all cares upon You and
please help me bear this and all burdens, in the name of Jesus Christ
our Lord."

Brothers, let's not let our women bear those burdens. Honor her
as the weaker sex by acknowledging that she is the woman that God
has made and He wants us to give them great honor.

Women, do not attempt to bear those burdens on your own.. Take
them to your husband, fiancé, friend, or close male friend that you
can completely trust with God's help.

Women, completely submit yourself to your husband, even to the
extent of calling him lord if you can muster the strength, and know
that it is okay to do that as you keep your eyes on the Lord Jesus
Christ. Pray to the Lord for your men and whatever burden is on your
heart. Take it to the Lord in prayer with your husband.

When Hannah in 1 Samuel 1:2–17 was faced with the same
problem that Rachel had in being barren, childless, which the Bible
calls a reproach, shame, or disgrace and it being that way in the
nation of Israel for hundreds of years and in America also, Hannah,
after taking the problem to her husband, Elkanah, took it to "the
Tabernacle at Shiloh to make a vow" (covenant or promise). Do you
have a church home that you can go to worship our God or to give
Him a promise? And will you submit yourselves to your husbands?

Read what 1 Peter 2:21b-3:7 says. Christ who suffered for you is your example. Follow in his steps. He never sinned, and He never deceived anyone. He did not retaliate when He was insulted. When He suffered, He did not threaten to get even. He left His case in the hands of God, who always judges fairly. He personally carried our sins in His own body on the cross so we can be dead to sin and live for what is right. You have been healed by His wounds! Once you were wandering like lost sheep. But now you have turned to your Shepherd, the Guardian of your souls.

3:1 In the same way, you wife must accept the authority of your husbands, even those (husbands) who refuse to accept the Good News (the gospel). Your godly life will speak to them better than any words. They will be won over by watching your pure, godly behavior.

Don't be concerned about the outward beauty that depends on fancy hairstyles, expensive jewelry, or beautiful clothes. You should be known for the beauty that comes from within, the unfading beauty of a gentle and quiet spirit, which is so precious to God. That is the way the holy women of old made themselves beautiful. They trusted God and accepted the authority of their husbands. For instance, Sarah obeyed her husband, Abraham, when she called him her master (her lord, KJV). You are her daughters when you do what is right without fear of what your husbands might do.

In the same way, your husbands must give honor to your wives. Treat her with understanding as you live together. She may be weaker than you are, but she is your equal partner in God's gift of new life. (You have become one in Christ)

"If you don't treat her as you should, your prayers will not be heard" (NLT).

Verse 7, in the New Revised Standard Version, says "Husbands, in the same way, show consideration for your wives in your life together, paying honor to the woman as the weaker sex, since they too are also heirs of the gracious gift of life—so that nothing may hinder your prayers."

In this verse, it says "paying honor." You owe it to her. Let her know that you love her. Tell her and show it constantly. But that marriage before everything, yes, surely before your job, and wives put that marriage even before that baby or those children. Work at keeping your relationship warm with your wife. Fan that flame or don't get married. Remember, you owe her that honor. Make her feel really good as to who she is in your life in Christ.

A few days before the Oscar award, I spoke with Terrence and asked him if he was keeping abreast of what was happening in Hollywood and with the Oscars. He said, "Yes, and I want Denzel to win one." Because the movie having to do with a father being extremely concerned for his son's well-being is probably what prompted Terrence to choose Mr. Washington regarding receiving the award. Terrence was probably thinking about his son, little Terrence. He has not spent much time with him since he was three years old. He is now ten. He does spend an hour or so with him during the Christmas season. And last year, li'l Terrence had a birthday party that Terrence attended. I believe he is in much despair not being able to spend much time with his son. The child stays on my mind and in prayer with his dad all the time. God has given them to me as an inheritance. I know Terrence feels the same way regarding his son being his inheritance.

Well, Denzel Washington did win. I believe by the grace of God. I believe God meets us wherever we are in life, even in Hollywood, if the prayer of faith is being prayed for those people. They are God's people.

This Christian walk is a walk of humility, giving in the life of others and of course faith in the Lord Jesus Christ. Regarding humility, we see Mr. Washington humbling himself and giving honor to Sidney Potier, who received an honorary Oscar the same night that he won his Oscar. He humbled himself and said, "I have followed your steps for many years and will continue to."

Regarding my daughter, Ms. Berry, she gave accolades to other actresses who has gone before her. She said, "I received this award in honor of Cicely Tyson, Diann Carroll, Vivica Fox," and others that I believe she feels are as qualified as she is that are black and have not received an Oscar.

Also, regarding giving, Nicole Kidman's former spouse in an interview with Entertainment Tonight (ET) gave into her life when he told ET that he was supporting her. I went through a divorce before becoming a Christian, and it was no fun. Afterward, Terrence's mother and I did become friends again, but during one part of that divorce process, it was very hard for both of us. During that process, to think that she would not call me her friend would be an understatement. As for my daughter, Ms. Kidman, to have the support of her former spouse, Tom Cruise, was a grand thing. God will bless him because of that attitude.

As Ms. Berry received the Oscar, Ms. Kidman stood and applauded, commending her. They were both up for the same award I believe. Ms. Kidman is a great actress. I pray that she receives several Oscars in the future because of her attitude and her talent. In one of her first movies, I believe *Far and Away*, she appeared with Mr. Cruise. He had an accident or something that caused her to think he was dead. She allowed herself to suffer great stress in that scene, and I believe it got the attention of all her viewers. Other scenes similarly have made her great.

America, I love God's people and try to encourage them anytime that I can and believe that He would have me to because He loves them.

I'm reminded of Levi, the tax collector, whom the Jewish people hated because he stole from them, his own brothers and sisters. The Lord Jesus Christ won him over by preaching the truth and changed his name to Matthew. He became an apostle (one of the five ministries of a preacher) and wrote the Gospel of Matthew, the first Gospel in our New Testament. I believe God is going to bless many celebrities (politicians, people in the media, talk show hosts, and especially entertainers, those that are in film, music, comedy, and sports).

Many that are cast down, I believe, He is going to raise up. I also believe that process has started. Others who have waited for a long time for your name to be blessed. I believe He is going to bless your name, and when He does, it will be blessed forever. Nicole Kidman and many, many others. Mary, the mother of the Lord Jesus Christ, said, "All generations will call me blessed." You are probably thinking, "That's the mother of God Himself, you know her name will be remembered for ever." Well, consider Mary Magdalene and Rahab, who were both prostitutes that the Bible speaks against as the worst profession and sin and shame there is. God changed their lives and blessed their names forever. Rahab was (or is) the great-grandmother of Jesse who was the father of David.

Consider David! God took a thirteen, fourteen, or fifteen-year-old boy out of a sheep field, raised him up to be a great warrior so that he could kill a ten-foot-plus giant, and then raised him up to be that greatest king that had ever lived. Except the Lord Jesus Christ, He is the Lord of all Lords and the King of all Kings, God has set. Him above everybody and everything.

But consider Ruth who was not even in the family of the Israelites. God brought her from Moab, blessed her name, and named a book of the Bible after her.

Christ saints took a term very familiar to the world and made it great. The secular term is "Hall Mark Hall of Fame." The Christian term is "Hall Mark Hall of Faith." In the eleventh chapter of the book of Hebrews is a list of many of God's children who died in faith, and their names will live forever.

Again, my prayer and belief are that God is going to bless many celebrities. But I believe God is going to have to help you get to where you need to be in Christ. He should not have to help you and will not if you will only come to Him and repent. But that has not happened yet. Children, God loves you very much. He sent His only begotten Son to die on the cross. But the Bible says God chastens those that He loves.

We in this nation have removed God from all public settings. It seems that He is doing all that He can to show mercy and grace. It was impressed upon my heart that what happened on 9/11 could have happened simultaneous in every major city in this nation, but it did not happen. I believe God is showing us much long-suffering. The Bible says He is very long-suffering. But how long is He going to suffer the sin of America? He loves you! Do you believe it? Meet Him at your local church next Sunday. He's waiting to see you there.

America, I have prayed for many in this nation and other parts of the world. Two of the greatest people I've been led to pray for are Diana, Princess of Wales, and former President Bill Clinton, neither of which is mentioned in the letter. But they are listed among many other celebrities in a letter that I wrote to the ministers that I have served under, which is available to you.

God answering my prayer means a great deal to me, especially when I am praying for this nation and the people in this nation or key people and places in other parts of the earth.

I am a God-called preacher of the Gospel. I want to be God's great prophet and evangelist (or shepherd). Remember when King Hezekiah received the threatening letter from the boasting and arrogant King Sennacherib and the wicked person that skope for him.

Upon receiving the letter, he sent a message to the prophet Isaiah, asking the prophet to pray for him. We see Isaiah speaking a great word of prophecy to King Hezekiah.

God has answered many prayers that I prayed. There are times when I also have to speak for God. All that we do should be in line with His Word.

My prayer is that God will touch the heart of every person in this nation.

Christ our Lord said, "When the Son of Man returns, will He find faith in the earth?" Pray for your brothers and sisters in this nation. It doesn't matter what the color or creed. Use your faith in Christ and believe with me that He is going to minister (give) life (spiritual life by the Holy Spirit) to every person in this nation. We know that everyone is not going to heaven. Hell will be filled with people that Satan has deceived, but they do not have to be in this land. I am believing for a great revival or spiritual awakening.

I also believe God is helping us by bringing chastisement upon this land. Again, Hebrews 12:6a: "For whom the Lord loveth he chasteneth. (v 7a) If ye endure chastening, God dealeth with you as with sons."

Surely, America, you want Him to be your Heavenly Father. He has to allow all the things that are happening to us because we have sinned against Him, by taking prayer and Bible reading out of our schools and godliness out of all public settings. He is allowing the terrorist attacks, the bombings and attacks on our schools to get our attention. He wants us to turn back to Him! Do you believe it? Will you do it?

Also, regarding prayer, there are some challenges greater than others. In Matthew 21:21–21, the Lord gives us the authority to speak to mountains. He uses mountains because they are obstacles that cannot be moved by mere man. But with His authority and speaking in His name, these mountains (cancer, AIDS, lupus, any terminal disease) or any obstacle can be moved, job-related problems, marital problems, or any surmountable difficulty that refuses to move by mere man.

In these verses, Jesus says, "If you have faith and doubt not, ye (you) shall not only do this which is done to the fig tree, but also if ye shall say unto this mountain, be thou removed, and be thou cast into the sea; it shall be done. And all things, whatsoever ye shall ask in prayer, believing, ye shall receive."

So not only do we see Him giving us the authority to speak to mountains, we also see in verse 22 that we should ask in prayer, believing.

In addition to speaking to mountains and asking in prayer, He has also given the authority to curse these obstacles (such as deadly diseases). In verse 21, He says, "Ye shall not only do this which is done to the fig tree." He had cursed the fig tree in verse 19 of this chapter. Some say that He had Israel or its religious leaders in mind when He did this, because they, like this fig tree, did not bear fruit.

Now regarding these same obstacles, the natural instances we see in the Old Testament, we make spiritual applications in our lives, during this New Testament (or dispensation of grace) in which we live.

In the Old Testament, we see David, a thirteen-, fourteen-, or fifteen-year-old lad taking on a giant approximately ten feet tall.

This was a natural or real occurrence in David's life, but we make a spiritual application.

As David took on and defeated Goliath, the giant, with God's help, as recorded in 1 Samuel 17:24–51, we make spiritual application by acknowledging the Word of God that says, "God is the same yesterday, today and forever." The things that He did yesteryear in David's life, He will do today in our lives. The Word of God also declares that "God is no respector of persons," meaning He doesn't love David or the men of old any more than He loves us. We have to believe that.

We do have to show our faithful to God just as these faithful ones in the Old and New Testaments have done, and I feel confident in believing that God is moving mightily in our lives (mine in particular) regarding us taking on giants (large problems).

The Bible says that when David took on the giant, "he chose five smooth stones." He only needed one for that giant. It's been said Goliath had four other brothers.

As we see God helping us defeat giants in our lives, we also believe that He is going to help with all other obstacles, mountains, and giants to come.

Because this nation has turn its back to God by taking prayer and Bible reading out of our schools and by taking godliness out of all public settings, I see all of our systems in this nation as giants that I must confront in prayer and in any other way that I can, for the betterment of all the people of this nation according to the Constitution of the United States, which were founded on godly principle by our Founding Fathers and their faith in the Lord Jesus Christ.

As young adults, we in the black community heard many times that the IRS were doing all that it could to put black celebrities in prison on tax evasion charges. We also saw IRS employees boasting about coming after and putting people in jail just because they had the authority. I personally witnessed these things occurring during the sixties and seventies. As I heard of these threats, fear began to grip my heart. When I became a Christian in 1981, I received a prayer power that was (and is) unshakable. After the fear of the IRS attacking me over the years, upon becoming a Christian I asked Christ to help me with this fear and all fears, and He did. I could sense the power of the Holy Spirit rising up inside of me when this fear would come.

In 1993–94 in Garland, Texas, in the bedroom of my son Terrence's home of which I was living at the time, in prayer that giant was confronted and defeated. A few years later, President Clinton made some changes in the Internal Revenue System (IRS). He stated that the system and the employees of the system will begin to work with the people to resolve any issues regarding taxes. The problem was not resolved when he made those changes in our laws. The issue was resolved in prayer months before that by God Almighty.

Because prayer has been taken out of our schools with Bible reading and because the Supreme Court and the leaders of our nation have misinformed God's people regarding church and state, I consider our school system as a giant. I consider our political system to be a giant that's hurting God's people by taken godliness out of all public settings. Each time we have city council meeting in this nation, it should be open with a word of encouragement from God's Holy Scriptures and in prayer.

I thank God for former mayor Ron Kirk, Dallas's first black mayor. The time that I tuned in to Dallas City Council Meeting he requested that a minister of the Gospel open the meeting in prayer. Ron Kirk is now running for state senator. I pray that he makes it. We in Christianity are praying for God to raise up more godly government leaders.

Each time there is a meeting regarding the governing of God's people in this nation, it should be opened in prayer asking Him to help govern His people and asking Him for the wisdom to know how to govern His people. We need Him, America. It's going to get worse in this nation and throughout the earth. We are not coming to an end of the age (dispensation) we are there, and Christ will soon return together. His Bride (the Body of Christ), His church.

Regarding these meetings, the leaders of our nation should do all they can to lead God's people back to Him, and it should be done at every level: city, state, and national and in every meeting.

Even the banking system is involved in this "one world order," and it seems the banking system is topping the list with our school system regarding major problems. I read a book entitled *Wake America, It's Later Than You Think*. This book tells of a few very wealthy men (bureaucrats) who are trying to come together for the expressed purpose of controlling the entire earth through the banking system, which of course means our banks would be involved as well.

Again, every system in our nation has become a giant, terrifying God's people. God is helping us (ministers) and all Christians (myself in particular) to confront every giant.

When David asked King Saul for permission to fight the giant, Goliath, Saul told him he was only a boy and would be no match for the giant. David's reply was "When I tended my father's flock, a lion and bear tried to kill the sheep, but I smote them and when they tried to rise up against me, I killed them. The same God that was with me when I killed the lion and the bear is going to be with me to deliver unto me the head of this giant."

I have to believe, America, the same God that was with me to help me confront the IRS will be with me regarding all the systems in America that have turned their backs to God.

As David chose five smooth stones for other giants, we in Christianity choose the Word of God. It, too, is a stone. The Bible says it is a solid rock, the rock of our salvation. It keeps us from all harm and danger. And that Word has become flesh and now dwells among us.

In the Gospel of Luke, the first chapter, we see an angel, Gabriel, sent to give Mary a word from the Lord. The angel told her she would be with child. She asked, "How can this be, seeing I know not a man?" (a virgin). The angel answered and said unto her, "The Holy Ghost shall come upon thee and the power of the Highest shall overshadow thee: there fore also that Holy thing which shall be born of thee shall be called the Son of God."

When the angel, Gabriel, gave her the word that was sent from God, she only had what is expected from all of us, and that is faith in God or His Word. Her reply to the angel was "Be it unto me according to thy word." God expects the same thing of us, America. Can you believe in the virgin birth? Can you believe the word that was given to Mary by the angel from God became flesh, simply, only, because she believed it when it was given to her? Can you believe Jesus Christ is God manifested in the flesh?

It takes faith to believe, and Hebrews 11:6 says, "Without faith it is impossible to please Him, for he that cometh to God must believe that He is, and that He is a rewarder of them that diligently seek Him." God wants us to have faith in Him. He also wants to reward us for having and using our faith to diligently seek Him.

February 6, 2002

The primary purpose for this writing is to bring our nation back as one nation under God and to join Dr. Noah Hutchings and Southwest Radio Church in sounding the alarm.

Regarding bringing our nation back under God, I sometimes feel as if I shoul sue our Supreme Court. In the past, the courts always use precedents to base their decisions on their finding. For example, again, we see this ruling by the US Supreme Court in 1892, the *Church of the Holy Trinity v United States.* The Court said, "No purpose of action against religion can be imputed to any legislation, state or nation, because this is a religious people . . . This is a Christian nation."

What would lead the courts to believe that we were a Christian nation? This case was not long. It was only sixteen pages in the court records. But the court provided eighty-seven precedents to support its conclusion. The court quoted the Founding Fathers. The court quoted the acts of the Founding Fathers. The Court quoted the acts of Congress. The court quoted the acts of the state government, and others. At the end of eighty-seven precedents, the court explained that it could have continued to cite many additional precedents but that certainly eighty-seven were sufficient to conclude that we were a Christian nation.

When prayer and Bible reading were removed from our schools in 1962–63, the court used no precedents. This is very important because the courts based their decisions on precedents. The courts always go back and examine both history and rulings from previous cases, so the court can be consistent in its present ruling. But when prayer and Bible reading were taken out, there were no precedents used. Why? Is that illegal? I'm sure that prayer and Bible reading had kept this nation in tack.

There are many other nations that have changed their form of government, such as France, which has changed its form of government seven times in the last two hundred years. Italy is on its fifty-first. Yet we in America is still on our first because of God's grace toward us and our dedicated faith and service to Him, putting no other god before Him. George Washington, the Father of our nation, said, "No one could be called an American patriot, who ever attempted to separate politics from its two foundations." He pointed out in his farewell address that the two foundations for political prosperity in America were religion and morality. And that no one (being Buddhas worshippers, Islam, or believer of any other god) could call themselves an American patriot. That includes American Indians (Native Americans) as well if they do not believe in or worship God our Father and the Lord Jesus Christ.

If you are a practicing Buddhist or Islamist, you know that our nation was founded on Christian principles when the Pilgrims, a group of Puritans that loved God so much, came to this nation to get from under the rule of King James in England, declaring "We want to bow to know one but God of Father and the Lord Jesus Christ." Even before our Founding Fathers founded this nation in 1776, the Pilgrims (Puritans) established it centuries before.

It is being said that our history is no longer being taught in public schools. Well, it should be so that Buddhist, Islamists, and all other religion worshipers may gain the knowledge of the "one true God."

In his farewell address, President Washington stated, "Of all the dispositions and habits which led to political prosperity, religion and morality are indispensable supports. In vain would that man claim the tribute of patriotism, who should labor to subvert these great pillars."

Remember this was always the threat of France and England coming against our Founding Fathers and this nation. Washington is saying, "If we cannot depend on you given your life for your nation, you cannot be called a patriot. And if you cannot be called a patriot, you should not be in this nation bowing before other gods." He probably is saying you should not be in this nation. Why would you want to be here, knowing on our US currency we declare "In God We Trust."

The other reason for this writing, which is even more important, is to "sound the alarm." Not only for our nation, the US, but this alarm is for young William, young Harry (our royal sons), Princess Stephany, Princess Caroline (our royal daughters), Sarah Ferguson (our duchess), and all of Wales, England, Scotland, and the British Commonwealth of Nations. It is for Andrea Radigan, her Olympic teammates with Nadia Comaneci, and their homeland of Romania. It's for the Rivers Dancers and their homeland of Ireland. It's for Steffi Graf, Katarina Witt and their homeland of Germany. It is for the leader and spouse of France and their nation, and all other nations of the world.

Naturally speaking, we all are in trouble. Spiritually speaking, those that are Christian we are blessed. I count it an honor and a blessing to live in and be a part of this generation. For those that are not Christian, you do not want to be in this earth during the Great Tribulation. We are entering into a one world order. I would like to invite everyone to view the movie *Apocalypse* by Dr. Jack Van Impee and also the movie *Left Behind* by Tim LaHaye and Jerry B. Jenkins.

The tribulation is the last seven-year period in the earth that will usher in the Second Coming (second advent) of the Lord Jesus Christ. The Great Tribulation is the last half (three and a half years) of that seven-year period. During this period, there will be many wars. They will all lead to and climax with that great battle called the battle of Armageddon.

In the late fifties to early sixties, there was great fear in our nation. The threat of Russia wiping the US off the face of the globe was spoken about in the news continually—on television, in the newspapers and magazines as well. It was constantly broadcasted that all the Russian leader needed to do was to press a simple little button and we in America would be completely destroyed. We were told in the US that our president, J. F. Kennedy was equipped with the same ability with which he had the authority to press a similar button and completely annihilate Russia. But we, especially myself being a child, were very afraid.

When Russia positioned one of its vessels near the US, bound for Cuba, President J. F. Kennedy called their bluff and made them back down and turn that ship around because it might have had missiles on it, and with Cuba being only ninety miles from our Florida coast and an ally of Russia, he would not permit it. The US was proud of our president. But the fear factor was still there. Being a child, I can still remember how afraid I was then. I believe that same fear is in our nation now. As I consider the state our nation is in, I believe conditions are going to get progressively worse as for that fear factor. The Bible says that man's heart is going to fail because of fear. No matter what is happening, I have to consider that we have entered into the end times. Therefore, it is always with me, the fact that there will be wars and rumors of wars (Matt. 24:6).

THE FUTURE OF OUR NATION

There is a movie entitled *Jesus* mailed to homes throughout the US. It is a very good movie because it was taken directly from Luke's Gospel. In this movie Jesus was the guest of Zacchaeus. Zacchaeus stood and said unto the Lord, "Behold, Lord, the half of my goods I give to the poor; and if I have taken anything from any man by false accusation, I restore him fourfold." And Jesus said unto him, "This day is salvation come to this house, forasmuch as he also is a son of Abraham." As Jesus spoke the words, one could see that something else was on his mind so intensely you could see it in his face. He was on His way to Jerusalem to die on the cross for the sin of all mankind (Luke 19:1–10).

As time goes on and we continue to enter into what we know as the last days, I believe it will become progressively more unsettled, even fearful as time continues in our land and through the earth. But those that have accepted the Lord Jesus Christ as Savior, He has promised to give them peace. He says "These things

ALVIN R. ERVIN

China--The Lion Roars

I have spoken unto you that in Me you might have peace. In the world you shall have tribulation: but be of good cheer; I have overcome the world. (John 16:33)

Christ also says, "Come unto me, all you that labour and are heavy laden, and I will give you rest. Take My yoke upon you, and learn of Me; for I am meek and lowly in heart: and you shall find rest unto your souls. For My yoke is easy, and my burden is light" (Matt. 11:28–30).

The fear that was in this nation during the late fifties and early sixties is coming upon us now.

The incident that we had with China a few months ago will probably lead to something greater in the future. The Bible says that "200 million soldiers" will come from the East. See page 4 of May 2001 issue of Southwest Radio Church Ministries *Prophetic Observer*: "Even newspapers in China now predict a war with the United States. China cannot match (yet) the US in modern weapons and technology. For example, the US has 18 times as many nuclear missiles." What China has is many more times of is men. According to Revelation 9:14–16, an army of 200 million soldiers will cross the Euphrates from the East to fight at the battle of Armageddon.

Not only are these threats not going to cease, they are going to intensify, getting progressively worse. I have received newsletters from Southwest Radio Church Ministries since the mid-eighties. At the upper-left corner of all their envelopes and at the top of each *Prophetic Observer* are the words "Go, set a watchman, let him declare what he seeth" (Isa. 21:6). Joel 2:1 says, "Blow ye the trumpet in Zion, and sound an alarm in my holy mountain: let all the inhabitants of the land tremble: for the day of the Lord cometh, for it is nigh (near) at hand."

It is time for the American people to know what is ahead of them. Please consider this information taken from *The Bible Knowledge Commentary, New Testament* by Dallas Seminary Faculty (NIV), pages 947 and 966 (BKCNT):

"The future world government begins with a time of peace" (tribulation period, the first three and a half years) "but is soon followed by destruction" (1 Thess. 5:3). In general, the seals, trumpets, and bowls of divine wrath signal the terrible judgments of God on the world at the end of the Age, climaxing in the Second Coming of Christ" (page 947 BKCNT).

We will not deal with the opening of the seven seals, nor the sounding of seven trumpets, but I will deal the seven bowls of divine wrath in Revelation chapter 16.

The Bowls of Divine Wrath

Chronologically, this chapter is close to the time of the Second Coming of Christ, and the judgments described fall in rapid succession (all twenty-one events). "Alford says, 'There can then be no doubt here, not only that the series reaches on to the time of the end, but that the whole of it is to be placed close to the same time'" (The Greek Testament, 4:696). Daniel indicated that these closing of the tribulation will be a time of world war (Dan. 11:36–45). World events are now pictured by John as rapidly coming to their climax (page 966).

The First Bowl

John recorded that he heard a loud voice from the temple instructing the seven angels to pour out the seven bowls of God's wrath on the earth. This is undoubtedly the voice of God speaking from His heavenly temple. The adjective translated "loud" (megalés) is frequently used in this chapter (v 17 also refers to the loud voice). But the same Greek word is used in connection with intense heat (v 9), the great river Euphrates (v 12), the great day of God Almighty (v 14), a severe earthquake (v 18), the great city (v 19), Babylon the Great (v 19), huge hailstones (v 21), and a terrible plague (v 21). The judgments being poured out are greater, more severe, more intense than anything that has happened in the preceding events. When the first angel . . . poured out his bowl of wrath, it produced ugly and painful sores on those who had the beast's mark and worshipped his image. (16:1–2)

The question has been raised as to whether the bowls of the wrath of God are chronologically subsequent to or identical with the seven trumpets of the angels. There is clearly much similarity between the trumpet judgments and the bowl judgments. They both deal with (a) the earth (8:7) or the land (16:2), (b) the sea (8:8; 16:3), (c) the rivers and springs of water (8:10; 16:4), and (d) the sun, moon, and stars (8:12) with only the sun mentioned in the bowl judgments (16:8–9). The fifth trumpet dealt with demon possession with the sun and sky darkened (9:1–3), which is similar to the fifth bowl in which darkness will cover the earth and sores will cause agony among men (16:10–11). The sixth trumpet deals with the river Euphrates

(9:13–14), and the sixth bowl will dry up the Euphrates (16:12). The seventh trumpet implies that the Great Tribulation is coming to its end (11:15–19), and the seventh bowl of the wrath of God records a loud voice from heaven, saying, "It is done!" (16:17) with resulting destruction of the earth by earthquake and hail, which is also included in the seventh trumpet (11:18–19).

Similarities, however, do not prove identity, and a comparison of the trumpets with the bowls of God's wrath reveals striking differences even though the order of the judgments is the same. In the trumpet judgments, generally speaking, a third of the earth or heaven is afflicted, whereas in the bowl judgments the effects of the judgments are on the entire earth and are much more severe and final in character. Accordingly, it seems best to follow the interpretation which has long been held in the church that the seven bowls are an expansion of the seventh trumpet, just as the seven trumpets are an expansion of the breaking of the seventh seal. The order is climactic, and the judgments become more intensive and extensive as the time of the Second Coming of Christ approaches. All indications are that the bowl judgment fall with trip-hammer rapidity on a world that is reeling under previous judgments and a gigantic world war. Some bowl judgments are selective and extend only to the wicked (16:2, 8–11), and several affect parts of natural (sea, rivers, sun, etc.).

In the first bowl judgment, people who followed the Antichrist received painful sores. Sores also come with the fifth bowl (vv 10–11).

The Second Bowl

16:3. After the second trumpet blew (8:8–9), "a third of the sea turned into blood," killing "a third of the living creatures" and destroying "a third of the ships" (8:8–9). In the second bowl, however, every living thing in the sea died (16:3). It is probable that the ocean here did not chemically correspond to human blood, but that it looked like blood and had the same effect in killing everything. Just as in the second trumpet, the blood here is analogous to the first plague in Egypt (Ex. 7:20–25). As most of the earth's surface is covered by the seas, this is a worldwide, tremendous judgment.

The Third Bowl

16:4–7. Just as the third trumpet made "a third of the waters" bitter (8:11), so the third bowl extends the judgment of the second bowl on the sea to rivers and springs, and they became blood (16:4). John heard the angel in charge of the waters proclaim that God the Holy One is just in His judgments (v 5). For God's work in turning the waters to blood is in response to the shedding of the blood of saints and prophets (v 6). This is echoed by a word from the altar declaring the judgment just (v 7; cf. 15:3).

The Fourth Bowl

16:8–9. This judgment focused the intense heat of the sun. In response, people cursed God and refused to repent (cf. v 11), By contrast, the fourth trumpet (8:12) darkened a third of the heavens but did not include additional intense heat. It is clear from this and other prophecies that dramatic changes in climate will occur in the Great Tribulation.

The Fifth Bowl

16:10–11. This judgment was directed toward the beast's throne, imposed darkness on the earth, and inflicted painful sores (cf. v 2) on people. Again, they cursed God and refused to repent. This is the last reference in Revelation to a failure to repent (cf. 2:21; 9:21; 16:9; cf., however, 16:21). The fifth bowl is similar to the fifth trumpet (9:1–11) in that both will bring darkness, but the fifth trumpet has to do with demon possession rather than physical pain.

The Sixth Bowl

16:12. According to John's revelation, the sixth angel poured out his bowl and dried up the river Euphrates to prepare the way for the kings from the East. There has been endless speculation about the kings from the East, "with many expositors trying to relate them to some contemporary leaders of their generation." A survey of one hundred commentaries of the book of Revelation reveals at least fifty interpretations of the identity of the kings of the East. The simplest and best explanation, however, is that this refers to kings or rulers from the Orient or East who will participate in the final world war.

In light of the context of this passage indicating the near approach of the Second Coming of Christ and the contemporary world situation in which the Orient today contains a large portion of the world's population with tremendous military potential, an interpretation other than a literal one does not make sense. Alford states it concisely,

"This is the only understanding of these words which will suit the context, or the requirement of this series of prophecies" (Alford, *The Greek Testament*, 4:700).

This is related to the great river Euphrates because this is the water boundary between the Holy Land and Asia to the East (cf. comment on 9:12–16). While the implication is that the water is dried up by an act of God, the fact is that dams have been built across the Euphrates River in this century to divert water for irrigation so that there are times even today when there is little or no water in in the Euphrates. The Euphrates River is frequently mentioned in scripture (e.g., Gen. 15:18; Deut. 1:7; 11:24; Josh. 1:4). The drying up of this river is also predicted in Isaiah 11:15.

16:13–16. John was then given a symbolic and comprehensive view of the preparation for the final bowl of God's wrath. He saw three evil spirits that looked like frogs coming out of the mouths of Satan (the dragon) and the two beasts (the Antichrist [13:1–10] and the false prophet [13:11–18]). One need not speculate on the identity of the three frogs, for verse 14 explains that they are spirits of demons performing miraculous signs. These demons go throughout the world influencing kings to assemble for the battle on the great day of God Almighty ("Almighty" [the greek word, pantokrator] is also used in 1:8; 4:8; 11:17; 15:3; 16:7; 19:6, 15; 21:22).

While the meaning of this symbolic presentation is clear, there is a major problem involved in what the demons do. The coming world government in the Great Tribulation will be established by the power of Satan (13:2). Here, however, Satan, the world ruler, and the false prophet unite in inciting the nations of the world to gather for the final world war. Actually, the war is a form of rebellion against the world ruler. Why then should satanic forces be let loose to destroy the world empire that has just been created?

The answer seems to be in the events that follow. Satan, knowing that the Second Coming of Christ is near, will gather all the military might of the world into the Holy Land to resist the coming of the Son of Man (Jesus Christ our Lord), coming of a thief. It implies suddenness and unpreparedness as far as unbelievers are concerned. Just as Christians are not to be surprised by the Rapture of the church (1 Thess. 5:4), so believers at the time of the Second Coming will be anticipating His return. Blessing is promised to the one who is prepared for the coming of the Lord by being attired in the righteousness or clothing that God Himself supplies.

Taken as a whole, the sixth bowl of the wrath of God is preparation for the final act of judgment before the Second Coming and is the later stage of development related to the river Euphrates, anticipated earlier (Rev. 9:14). The time factor between the sixth trumpet and the sixth bowl is comparatively short.

The Seventh Bowl

16:17–20. The seventh angel then poured out his bowl into the air. John heard a loud voice from the throne, saying, "It is done!" A similar pronouncement followed the seventh trumpet (11:15–19). Here also John saw lightning flashes and heard thunder, which was followed by a severe earthquake (16:18). John was then informed that this will be the greatest earthquake of all time (other earthquakes are mentioned) in 8:5 and 11:19, and the resulting description indicates that it will affect the whole earth with the possible exception of the land of Israel. The great city that split into three parts refers to the destruction of Babylon. The most important event, however, is that the cities of the nations collapsed. The huge earthquake will reduce to rubble all the cities of the nations (Gentiles). The stage is thus being set for the Second Coming of Christ. Obviously in the collapse of the world's cities there will be tremendous loss of life and destruction of what is left of the world empire.

Though Jerusalem is mentioned in 11:8 as "the great city," which is figurative called Sodom and Egypt, where also their Lord was crucified, "the great city" here is specifically Babylon, as indicated in 16:19. God will give Babylon the cup filled with the wine of the fury of His wrath—that is, she will experience a terrible outpouring of His judgment. Some have suggested that this city is Rome but is called Babylon because of its spiritual declension. While this has been debated at length by scholars (cf. J. A. Seiss, *The Apocalypse*, pp. 381–82, 397–420), it is preferable to view Babylon as the rebuilt city of Babylon located on the Euphrates River, which will be the capital of the final world government (cf. Walvood, *Revelation*, pp. 240–41).

In addition to the terrible earthquake and probably because of it, John recorded, "Every island fled away and mountains could not be found." These verses (vv 18–20), if taken literally, indicate topographical changes in the earth, which eventually will also include great changes in the Holy Land in preparation for Christ's millennial kingdom.

16:21. In addition to the earthquake, huge hailstones of about one hundred pounds each fell on people. Such huge masses of ice supernaturally formed would destroy anything left standing from the earthquake and would no doubt kill or seriously injure those they hit. In spite of the severity of the judgment and its cataclysmic character, the hardness of human hearts is revealed in the final sentence. And they cursed God on account of the plague of hail, because the plague was so terrible.

The Relationship of the Seals, Trumpets, and Bowls

<<<IMAGE>>>

"The question is sometimes raised why eternal punishment is eternal. The answer is that people in the hardness of their hearts will not change; they deserve eternal punishment." Eternal punishment because they are eternally unrepentant. "With the final destruction coming from the seventh bowl of the wrath of God, the stage will then be set for the dramatic and climactic Second Coming of Christ, revealed in chapter 19. Before this event, however, a future detailed description is given of Babylon in chapters 17–18."

The Fall of Babylon (Chapters 17–18)

> "Babylon—the source of so many heathen and pagan religions which have opposed the faith of Israel as well as the faith of the church—is here seen in its final judgment. These chapters do not fall chronologically within the scheme of the seals, trumpets, and bowls of the wrath of God."

In general, however, in chapter 17, Babylon is seen in its religious character climaxing in a world religion that seems to fit the first half of the tribulation period. Chapter 17 also record the destruction of Babylon by the 10 kings (v 16).

Chapter 18 by contrast, seems to refer to Babylon as a political power and as a great city and as the seat of power of the great world empire which will dominate the second half of the last seven years before Christ's return. Babylon, referred to about 300 times in the Bible, is occasionally viewed as a satanic religious program opposing the true worship of God, but primarily it is viewed as a political power with a great city bearing the name Babylon as its capital. The end times bring together these two major lines of truth about Babylon and indicate God's final judgment on it.

Religious Babylon Destroyed

17:1–2 "One of the seven angels (in chap. 16) who had one of the seven bowls invited John to witness the punishment of the great prostitute, who sits on many waters. This evil woman symbolizes the religious system of Babylon, and the waters symbolize "people, multitude, nations, and languages" (v 15). The angel informed John that the kings of the earth had committed adultery with the woman; in other words, they had become a part of the religious system which she symbolized (cf. 14:8).

17:3–5 John was then taken in the Spirit (or better, "in [his] spirit," i.e., in a vision, not body; cf. 1:10; 4:2) to a desert where he saw the woman herself. She was sitting on a scarlet beast that was covered with blasphemous names. The beast had seven heads and ten horns. The beast is an obvious reference to the world government (13:1). The ten horns are later defined (17:12) as ten kings who had "not yet received a kingdom." The seven heads seem to refer to prominent rulers of the yet future Roman Empire.

The woman was dressed in purple and scarlet, and was glittering with gold, precious stones, and pearls. Her adornment is similar to that of religious trappings of ritualistic churches today. While purple, scarlet, gold, precious stones, and pearls can all represent beauty and glory in relation to the true faith, here they reveal a false religion that prostitutes the truth."

"In her hand the woman held a golden cup . . . filled with abominable things and the filth of her adulteries" (cf. "the wine of her adulteries" in v 2). This confirms previous indications that her character and life are symbolic of false religion, confirmed by the words written on her forehead: Mystery Babylon the Great the Mother of Prostitutes and of the Abominations of the Earth. The NASB and NIV Bible are probably right in separating the word *mystery* from the title which follows because the word *mystery* is not part of a title itself. It describes the title."

The Bible is full of information about Babylon as the source of false religion, the record beginning with the building of the tower of Babel (Gen. 10–11). The name "Babel" suggests "confusion" (Gen. 11:9). Later the name was applied to the city of Babylon, which itself has a long history dating back to as early as three thousand years before Christ. One of its famous rulers was Hammurabi (1728–1686 BC). After a period of decline, Babylon again rose to great heights under Nebuchadnezzar about six hundred years before Christ. Nebuchadnezzar's reign (605–562 BC) and the subsequent history of Babylon is the background of the Book of Daniel."

"Babylon was important not only politically but also religiously. Nimrod, who founded Babylon (Gen. 10:8–12), had a wife known as Semiramis who founded the secret religious rites of the Babylonian mysteries, according to accounts outside the Bible. Semiramis had a son with an alleged miraculous conception who was given the name Tammuz and in effect was a false fulfillment of the promise of the seed of the woman given to Eve (Gen. 3:15)."

"Various religious practices were observed in connection with this false Babylonian religion, including recognition of the mother and child as God and of creating an order of virgins who became religious prostitutes. Tammuz, according to the tradition, was killed by a wild animal and then restored to life, a satanic anticipation and counterfeit of Christ's resurrection. Scripture condemns this false religion repeatedly (Jer. 7:18; 44:17–19, 25; Ezek. 8:14). The worship of Baal is related to the worship of Tammuz."

After the Persian took over Babylon in 539 BC, they discouraged the continuation of the mystery religions of Babylon. Subsequently, the Babylonian cultists moved to Pergamam (or Pergamos) where one of the seven churches of Asia Minor was located (cf. Rev. 2:12–17). Crowns in the shape of a fish head were worn by the chief priests of the Babylonian cult to honor the fish god. The Crowns bore the words "Keeper of the Bridge," symbolic of the "bridge" between man and Satan. This handle was adopted by the Roman emperors who used the Latin title Pontifex Maximus, which means "Major Keeper of the Bridge," and the same title was later used by the bishop of Rome.

The pope today is often called the pontiff, which comes from pontifex. When the teachers of the Babylonian mystery religions later moved from Pergamum to Rome, they were influential in paganizing Christianity and were the source of many so-called religious rites that have crept into ritualistic churches. Babylon then is the symbol of apostasy and blasphemous substitution of idol-worship for the worship of God in Christ. In this passage Babylon comes to its final judgment.

"17:6. The woman symbolizing the apostate religions system, was drunk with the blood of the saints. This makes it clear that the apostate religious system of the first half of the last seven years leading up to Christ's Second Coming will be completely devoid of any true Christians. As a matter of fact, the apostate church will attempt to kill all those who follow the true faith. John expressed his great astonishment at this revelation."

17:7–8. The angel explained the meaning of the woman and of the beast she was riding. The beast will come up out of the Abyss, the home of Satan (11:7) and the place from which demons come (9:1–2).

This indicates that the power behind the ruler is satanic (cf. 13:4) and that Satan and the man he controls are closely identified. Their power is one. The fact that the beast was, now is not, and will come up in the future is another indication of what was introduced in 13:3. The supernatural survival and revival of both the world ruler and his empire will impress the world as being supernatural and will lead to worship of the beast and Satan (on the book of life common 3:5).

17:9–11. The angel informed John this calls for a mind with wisdom (cf. 13:18). The truth that is being presented here symbolically requires spiritual insight to be understood, and the difficulty of correct interpretation is illustrated by the various ways it has been interpreted in the history of the church.

The angel informed John that the beast's heads are seven hills on which the woman sits. Many ancient writers, such as Victorinus, who wrote one of the first commentaries on the book of Revelation, identified the seven hills as Rome, often described as "the city of seven hills." This identification has led to the conclusion this passage teaches that Rome will be the capital of the coming world empire. Originally Rome included seven small mountains along the Tiber River, and the hills were given the names Palatine, Aventine, Caelian, Equiline, Viminal, Quirimal, and Capitoline. Later, however, the city expanded to the north called Pincian. While Rome is often referred to as having seven hills or mountains, different writers do not necessarily name the same seven mountains.

A close study of the passage does not support the conclusion that this refers to the city of Rome. Seiss, for instance, offers extensive evidence that the reference is to rulers rather than to physical mountains (*The Apocalypse*, pp. 391–94). This is supported by the text which explains they are also seven kings (lit., "the seven heads are seven kings"). If the mountains represent kings, then obviously they are not literal mountains and refer not to a literal Rome but to persons.

This view is also supported by verse 10: Five have fallen, one is, the other has not yet come, but when he does come, he must remain for a little while. John was writing from his point of view in which five prominent kings of the Roman Empire had already come and gone, and one was then on the throne (probably Domitian, who caused the persecution that put John on the island of Patmos). The identity of the seventh king, the one to come after John's time, is unknown."

Verse 11 adds that the final world empire will be headed by an eighth king, the beast who once was, and now is not, belongs to the seven and is going to his destruction. The eighth king is obviously identical to the final world ruler, the man who heads up the final world empire destroyed by Christ at His Second Coming.

One possible explanation of the difference between the seventh and eighth beast is that the seventh beast itself is the Roman Empire marvelously revived in the end time, and the eight beast is its final ruler. These verses show that in the end time, particularly during the first half of the last seven years, there will be an alliance between the Middle East ruler (the Antichrist) and the apostate world church of that time. This will come to a head, however, at the midpoint of the seven years, when that political power becomes worldwide.

17:12–14. Verse 12 explains that the ten horns are ten kings. While many commentators have tried to identify ten successive kings in the past, the passage itself indicates that they are contemporaneous kings who are heads of the countries that will form the original alliance in the Middle East that will support the future world ruler. They will receive authority for one hour as kings along with the beast. While seven heads may be chronologically successive rulers of the Roman Empire who are singled out as prominent, the ten horns by contrast are contemporaneous with each other, and as the text indicates, they will receive political power for a brief time.

The ten kings will unite their power to support the beast (v 13), the Middle East ruler who will emerge in the end time and will make a covenant with Israel seven years before the Second Coming of Christ. Their antagonism to Christ is indicated throughout the entire seven years. And when Christ returns, these ten kings will war against Him but will be defeated (v 14). Interestingly Christ the Lamb is also the Lord of lords and Kings of Kings (cf. 1 Tim 6:15; Rev. 19:16).

17:15. Verse 1 stated that the woman "sits on many waters." These waters are now interpreted as people, multitudes; nations, and languages. This indicates that there will be one ecumenical world religious system, embracing all nations and languages.

17:16–18. The chapter closes with the dramatic destruction of the woman. The beast (the world ruler, the Antichrist) and the ten horns (ten kings) will hate the prostitute and will bring her to ruin. While the exact time of this event is not given in this passage, it would seem to occur at the midpoint of the seven years when the beast will assume the role of the world dictator by proclamation (Dan. 9:27; Matt. 24:15).

When the ruler in the Middle East takes on worldwide political power, he will also assume the place of God and demand everyone worships him or else be killed (cf. Dan. 11:36–38; 2 Thess. 2:4; Rev. 13:8, 15). The world church movement, which characterizes the first half of the seven years leading up to the Second Coming, is thus brought to an abrupt end. It will be replaced by the final form of world religion, which will be the worship of the world ruler, Satan's substitute for Christ.

This is part of God's sovereign purpose to bring evil leaders into judgment. For God has put it into their hearts to accomplish His purpose by agreeing to give the beast their power to rule, until God's words are fulfilled.

The final description of the woman is given in 17:18: The woman you saw is the great city that rules over the kings of the earth. The reference to the woman as a city is another link with ancient Babylon, this time regarded as a religious center for false religion. The apostate church represented by the woman was a combination of religious and political power. As stated in verse 5, the city and the woman are a "mystery" and are therefore a symbolic presentation. Verse 18, however, introduces the next chapter which seems to refer to Babylon more as a literal city than as a religious entity.

Political Babylon Destroyed (Chapter 18)

18:1–3. Further revelation on the destruction of Babylon was made by another angel coming down from heaven. This contrast with "one of the seven angels" mentioned in 17:1 and should not be confused with angelic representations of Christ. Angels do have great authority and often make pronouncements in the book of Revelation. The power and glory of this angel was such that the earth was illuminated by his splendor (18:1)."

"The angel's message is summarized: Fallen! Fallen in Babylon the Great! The question has been raised as to whether or not this is another view of the same destruction mentioned in 17:16–17. A comparison of chapters 17 and 18 reveals that these are different events. The woman in chapter 17 was associated with the political power but was not the political power itself and her destruction apparently brought no mourning from the earth. By contrast the destruction of Babylon in the eighteen chapter brings loud lamentation from the earth's political and economic powers. Instead of being destroyed and consumed by the 10 kings, here the destruction seems to come from an earthquake, and it is probable that this is an enlarged explanation of what was described in 16:19–21."

"What is pictured here is a large prosperous city, the center of political and economic life. The judgment of God makes it a home for demons and a haunt for every evil spirit, a haunt for every unclean and detestable bird. For all the nations have drunk the maddening wine of her adulteries. This false religion is like a drug that drives men to madness. While it brought riches to merchants, it is now doomed for destruction."

"18:4-8. Following the pronouncement of the angel, another voice from heaven instructed the people of God to leave the city so that they would escape the judgment to come on it (vv 4-5). Babylon will receive torture and grief commensurate with her glory and luxury, in which she boasted that she was a queen (v 7). Death, mourning, and famine, also fire, will come on the city in one day (v 8)"

"18:9-20. When kings who were involved with the city see its destruction they will be grieved, and will cry, Woe! Woe, O great city, O Babylon, city of power! (v 10) Merchants too will bemoan the city's downfall since they will no longer be able to carry on commerce with the city. The description in verses 12–13 indicates the great luxury and wealth of the city. This obviously refers to an economic and political situation rather than a religious one. The mourning of the merchants is similar to that of the kings: Woe! Woe, O great city . . . ! (v 16)."

Sea captains . . . sailors, and others in navigational occupations will lament in similar fashion: Woe! Woe, O great city . . . ! (v 19) All three groups—kings, merchants, and sailors—speak of her destruction and sudden: in one hour (vv 10, 17, 19). As the world mourns the destruction of Babylon, the saints (all Christians) are told to rejoice because God has judged her for the way she treated you (v 20).

18:21–24. The final and violent destruction of the city—harpists and musicians, flute players and trumpeters, and workmen of any trade (v 22)—will not be seen in the city again. Nor will there be light and joy of weddings (v 23). The reason for her judgment is that by her magic spell (pharmakeia; cf. 9:21), all the nations were led astray from God (18:23; cf. 17:2), and she was guilty of murdering prophets and saints (18:24; cf. 17:6).

"The question remains as to what city is in view here. A common view is that it refers to the city of Rome, because of the prominence of Rome as the seat of the Roman Catholic Church and the capital of the Ancient Roman Empire. Some find confirmation of this in the fact that the kings and sea merchants will be able to see the smoke of the burning of the city (18:9, 18)."

To further add to the confirmation of this is the fact that there will be a revived Roman Empire and the certainty of Rome gaining all the glory that is spoken of in the book of Revelation makes Rome worshipped by all nations.

Please join Dr. Noah Hutchings, Southwest Radio Church, and I as we consider New York City, New York, as being "Mystery Babylon," or join me as I consider Southwest Radio Church's *Prophetic Observer*, October 2001 Issue, page 4, as stated earlier in the writing.

Mystery Babylon

I have been to the Babylon on the Euphrates as restored by Saddam Hussein. This Babylon we know. It is no mystery. It cannot be the "Mystery Babylon" of Revelation 18. The Babylon of Revelation is the greatest commercial city that exists in the last days. In world importance, it is comparable to the Babylon of Nebuchadnezzar's day. Of Mystery Babylon of the end time, we read,

> And the kings of the earth, who have committed fornication and lived deliciously with her, shall bewail her and lament for her, when they shall see the smoke of her burning. Standing afar off for the fear of her torment, saying, Alas, alas that great city Babylon that mighty city! for in one hour is thy judgment come. And the merchants of the earth shall weep and mourn over her, for no man buyeth their merchandise anymore. (Rev. 18:9–11)

Southwest Radio Church Ministries

Prophetic Observer

It grieves my soul to even make a comparison between Revelation 18 and what happened to New York City on September 11, 2001. Nevertheless, the similarities are striking. New York City is the greatest commercial port city in the world. It is traditionally called "The Babylon on the Hudson." Across the bay is Babylon, New York, part of the metro complex. The fall of the Twin Trade Towers, symbols of world commerce, fell within one hour, and on television we saw thousands upon thousands around the world joining in mourning this awful tragedy. Many prophecies in the Bible are conditional, like Jonah's declaration, "Forty days and Nineveh will be destroyed." Nineveh repented, and the city was spared. New York City, or the entire nation, does not have to be Mystery Babylon.

It is true we have forsaken God in many ways. We no longer allow our children to pray and read the Bible in public schools. We have allowed the killing of the unborn. Few of our churches now preach the Lord Jesus Christ as both Savior and Creator of all things in heaven and on earth. We have become a sinful and wicked nation. But our time for repenting before God and seeking His forgiveness is short.

A Turning Point?

I was disturbed because the name of Jesus Christ was not mentioned or honored more in the prayers and ceremonies after the Manhattan tragedy. However, our president did seek help from God out of the scriptures. Many in Congress did attend a prayer service in the Capital Rotunda. Churches and individual Christians across the nation were called upon to pray and seek God's help and comfort, and it was so good to hear our people once again stand up and declare that it was good to be an American. Just maybe God will hear us as a nation, seeking His forgiveness, and help. If so, then those who died at the World Trade Towers and the Pentagon, why do you think it is called the Big Apple."

I love New York, California, surely Texas, all of this nation, but I love God much more and know only He can help us. I thank God for what happened on September 11, 2001, if it accomplished God getting the attention of His people. And I do not believe those people lost their lives in vain. The families should be comforted in that fact.

Hebrews 12:56–13 (Liv. Bible) says, "My son, don't be angry when the Lord punishes you. Don't be discouraged when He has to show you where you were wrong. (v 6) For when He punishes you, it proves that he loves you. When He whips you, it proves you really are His child (v 7). Let God train you for he is doing what any loving Father does for his children. Whoever heard of a son who was never corrected? (v 8) If God doesn't punish you when you need it as other fathers punishes their sons, then it means that you aren't really God's son at all—that you don't really belong in His family" (v 9).

Since we respect our fathers here on earth, though they punish us, should we not all the more cheerfully submit to the chastisement of our Heavenly Father and live forever.; For four plus decades, we have deprived our little ones, as well as high school and college (but especially grade school) a time of prayer and fellowship with their Heavenly Father and their Savior Christ Jesus, the right that they have had for two hundred plus years. God is judging us, and we have to get it right by humbling ourselves before Him. We're going to get it right, I pray.

Hebrews 12:5(b)–13 (Liv. KJV Bible) say "My son, don't despise the chastening of the Lord, nor faint when thou art rebuked of Him; (v 6) For whom the Lord loveth he chasteneth, and scourgeth every son whom He receiveth. (v 7) If you endure chastening, God dealeth with you as with sons; for what son is he whom the father chateneth not? (v 8) If God doesn't punish you when you need it as other fathers, then it means that you aren't really God's son at all—that you don't really belong in His family" (v 9).

Since we respect our fathers here on earth, though they punish us, should we not all the more cheerfully submit to God's discipline so that we can began really to live? (v 10) Our earthly fathers trained us for a few brief years, doing the best for us that they knew how, but God's correction is always right and for our best good, that we may share in His holiness.

v 11. Being punished isn't enjoyable while it is happening, it hurts! But afterward we can see the result, a quiet growth in grace and character.

v 12. So take a new grip with your tired hands, stand firm on your shaky legs, and mark out a straight, smooth path for your feet so that those who follow you, though weak and lame, will not fall and hurt themselves, but become strong.

America, I thank God for you and I am proud of you. You handled 9/11 well. Since you are reaching out in New York to help your brothers and sisters, it surely reduces the probability that you are Mystery Babylon. Our Heavenly Father really hates her because of what she did to innocent people, His people. Revelation 18:20 says "Rejoice over her" (when she is destroyed) "thou heavens and ye holy apostles and prophets; for God hath avenged you on her."

March 26, 2002

Finally, brethren, we will deal with chapter 13, which teaches us and brings together all things regarding the end of this world as we know it and will also be the end of this book.

I will use information from Vaughn Shatzer and Joan Veon's videos and suggest that you view and read their material. As a minister of Gospel and is responsible for the teaching that you receive from me as being what I believe God has given me to share with you, I must say be careful how you believe, what you believe, and who you believe. I support all that Vaughn Shatzer teaches in his video entitled *The New World Disorder*. I also support all information given by Joan Veon except one comment she makes in her video entitled *The Demise of the Constitution*. She says that we are supposed to be a republic, not a democracy. While I believe I know why she makes that statement, I still disagree with it.

The republic form of government declares that our leaders make all decision for the American people, while the democratic form of government declares each person's voice in this nation should be heard and the majority of those speaking should rule. It has been a term the American people have become very familiar with: "The majority rules." Where Ms. Veon may have problems is the fact that as we rapidly move into one world order, that form of government will be called "global democracy" or "one world democracy," which means that the American practice of capitalism, which has been declared to the American people by the Constitution of the US, which says the economic system in which the means of production and distribution are privately owned and operated for profit, originally under fully competitive conditions, or each person has a right to free enterprise. A Vietnamese became an American citizen and in the 1980s became, without any formal college education, a millionaire through free enterprise, buying foreclosure properties.

This form of government by the American people will be compromised (combined) with communism and/or socialism. We know that the communistic form of government is led by a dictator such as Hitler and socialism is similar in many ways. Thus, combining capitalism, socialism, and communism, it becomes what is known as global democracy. But the true form of democracy has kept this nation in that by God's grace for two hundred plus years. Me making this statement does not mean that I am a Democrat. I have never voted for a Democrat president candidate.

But I did vote for Ronald Reagan because I was afraid for the American hostages held by Iran. I thought Mr. Reagan was the best candidate to get them released. I also voted for the Bushes. It wasn't the easiest thing for me because I was brought up in a Baptist Christian Democrat family. When I told my mother in the eighties that I had voted for Mr. Reagan, she looked at me as if I had disowned our family. I told her that I was very concerned for those hostages because threats were being made by the individuals holding them stating they were going to kill those innocent people.

We have been told that Republicans are more conservative, which means tending to preserve established institutions and methods and to resist or oppose any changes in these, which is said also to be more Christian oriented, which was also why I voted for the Bushes. But I prayed for Mr. Clinton to become president because he made some statements to lead me to think that he would do many things to help this nation in a Christian way. I also thought he would do those things proclaiming the name of the Lord Jesus Christ, but that did not happen.

At this point in my life I do not consider myself a Democrat or Republican but a Christian who wants to see our nation blessed using whatever form of government that will bring that about. Systems were given by God to help us conduct good business practices.

Both Mr. Shatzer's and Ms. Veon's materials may be obtained through Southwest Radio Church Ministries (1-800-652-1144).

As I deal with chapter 13 of the book of Revelation, most of the information given will be taken from *The Bible Knowledge Commentary* by Dallas Theological Seminary Faculty. We may also use information taken from Dr. J. Vernon McGee Commentary. I honor him greatly.

This reading will not be for your enjoyment but for your survival, your eternal survival.

Chapter 13

The next prophetic event in God's calendar of events is the Rapture of the church in which all believers of Jesus Christ are supernaturally remove from this earth in a twinkling of an eye according to 1 Thessalonians 4:16–17.

Immediately following the Rapture, the seven-year tribulation period is ushered in. Hear what the Lord Jesus Christ says from Matthew 24:21: "For there shall be Great Tribulation, such as was not since the beginning of the world to this time, no, nor ever shall be." There will be an unprecedented time of horrendous tribulation coming upon this earth, according to the Son of God. If you think it's bad now, with all the violence, the abortion, the illegal drugs, the occult, the killer diseases, the killer storms, the radical homosexual and lesbian agenda, etc., you wait until the Holy Spirit, the restrainer, is taken out of the way and the man of sin is revealed. All hell is going to break loose. You do not want to be on earth after Christ raptures His bride, the church. What we are seeing now is a Sunday school picnic compared to the tribulation period.

Revelation, chapter 13, lays out for us the satanic new world order, which is a counterfeit of the true new world order under Jesus Christ during the thousand-year reign.

Revelation 13 is the mid point during the seven-year tribulation period in which Satan will set up a World Government, a World

Military, a World Religion, and a World Economic System. (Ms. Joan Veon's tape and books will shed more light on how the World Government is being structured.)

These world systems will be run and ruled by two ungodly and wicked men called beasts. We know them as the Antichrist and false prophet. Let's first look at how the Antichrist will set up a one world government during the tribulation period.

Verse 1 of chapter 13 says, "I stood upon the sand of the sea, and saw a beast rise up out of the sea, having seven heads and ten horns, and upon his horns ten crowns, and upon his heads the name of blasphemy." We know from the prophecies recorded in Daniel 7 that the beast is the infamous Antichrist that will rule the world.

Verse 2, "And the beast which I saw like a leopard, and his feet were as the feet of a bear, and his mouth as the mouth of a lion: and the dragon gave him his power, and his seat, and great authority."

We can see the beast in verse 2 that the Antichrist receives his power and seat (throne) and great authority from the dragon. We know the dragon is Satan himself according to Revelation 12:9.

The Bible Knowledge Commentary (BKC) gives us additional information regading the beast in chapter 13:1-2: "A beast coming out of the sea. His ten horns and seven heads, with ten crowns on his horns, depict the revived Roman Empire, which was also represented by the fourth beast of Daniel, which also had ten horns" (Dan. 7:7-8; cf. Rev. 13:3; 17:3, 7). In Revelation 13 and 17 the beast is the world ruler, whereas in Daniel 7 the little horn on the beast was the world ruler.

The fact that the beast comes out from the sea indicates that he is a Gentile, for the sea of humanity is involved as his source (cf. Rev. 17:15).

Many have said that the beast refers to some character in past history, but the context clearly refers to the final three and a half years before Christ's Second Coming. Under the control of this central ruler in the Middle East during the Great Tribulation will be ten nations (cf. Dan. 7:24, "The ten horns are ten kings"). (For discussion of various alternatives views, see Walvoord, *Revelation*, pp. 198–99.)

In Revelation 13:2 the beast was seen to gather in the symbolism of the three preceding empires—Greece (a leopard, cf. Dan. 7:6), Medo-Persia (a bear, cf. Dan 7:5), and Babylon (a lion, cf. Dan. 7:4). The power of the beast was derived from Satan himself: the dragon gave the beast his power and his throne and great authority (NIV).

The Fatal Wound of the Beast (13:3)

In this verse, we will see the Antichrist receiving a fatal wound to the head and Satan will supernaturally heal that wound. Paul Crouch with his son Matthew produced a movie entitled *The Omega Code*. While this movie depicts much of what is happening according to the Bible Code and may seem hard to understand, but if we know the Word of God we would also know that one of the leading character that receives a wound in the head, in this movie is the Antichrist. And the two prophets that were killed and raised to life in three days in this movie are God's two witnesses spoken of in Revelation 11:3–6, that "have power to shut heaven, that it rained not in the days of their prophecy: and have power over water to turn to blood, and to smite the earth with all plagues, as often as they will." (v 6) "We know that Elijah spoke, and from his word it did not rain for three and a half years. We know Moses turned water to blood when he cursed the Nile River and brought many plaques on Egypt because Pharaoh would not let the nation of Israel leave Egypt. Thus, the two prophets in the movie are Elijah and Moses.

Children of America (young and old), watch that movie as well as *Apocalypse* by Jack Van Impee and *Left Behind* by Tim LaHaye and Jerry B. Jenkins. Tell others what you think of these movies. They are very entertaining, but much more, they are prophetic. These things will occur.

13:3 (BKC) "The seven heads of the beast seem to represent important rulers, and one of them, probably the seventh, suffered a fatal wound caused by a sword" (v 14), which was subsequently healed, causing astonishment in the entire world.

Many have attempted to identify this beast as someone in the past or present who is to become the final world ruler. Among the suggestions have been Nero, Judas Iscariot, Mussolini, Hitler, Stalin, Kissinger, and many others, but such men obviously do not fit the details of this yet future ruler.

What is the meaning of the fatal wound that is healed? Two possibilities seem to fit this description. Alford, for instance, sees the deadly wound as the destruction of "the Roman pagan Empire" by "the Christian Roman Empire," thus making it a matter of history rather than prophecy (*The Greek Testament*, 4:675). The revival of the Roman Empire would then be its miraculous healing. Another plausible explanation is that the final world ruler receives a wound that normally would be fatal but is miraculously healed by Satan. While the resurrection of a dead person seems to be beyond Satan's power, we believe Satan will raise him from the dead and as he is raised to life no one on planet will be able to destroy (kill) him except The Lord Jesus Christ with the Word of His Mouth says the Word of God. Satat is extremely powerful but no match for Christ in any way. .

The important point is that the final world ruler comes into power obviously supported by a supernatural and miraculous deliverance by Satan himself.

The worship of Satan and the beast 13:4–6. The supernatural character of the beast makes him the object of worship along with Satan, the source of his power. It has always been Satan's purpose to receive the worship due to God alone, as stated in Isaiah 14:14: "I will make myself like the Most High." This is Satan's final form of counterfeit religion in which he assumes the place of God, the Father, and the beast or the world ruler assumes the roles of King of Kings as a substitute for Christ. This situation is probably introduced at the beginning of the last three and a half years when the Great Tribulation begins.

Recognizing the supernatural character of Satan and the ruler, the question is raised, Who is like the beast? Who can make war against him? (Rev. 13:4) This apparently explains how the beast could become world ruler without a war. His blasphemous assumption of the role of God continues for forty-two months, during which time he blasphemes God as well as heaven and those who live in heaven.

The Worldwide Power of the Beast

13:7–8. The beast becomes a worldwide ruler, for his authority extends over every tribe, people, language, and nation. As predicted in Daniel 7:23, he does "devour the whole earth, trampling it down and crushing it."

"In addition to achieving political domination over the entire world, he also abolishes all other religion and demands that everyone worship him" (cf. 2 Thessalonians 2:4). All inhabitants of the earth worship the beast except those whose names are recorded in the book of life. In the expression the Lamb that was slain from the Creation of the world, the words "from the Creation of the world" seem, as in the NIV margin, to relate to the time in eternity past when the names were written in the book of life, rather than to Christ's crucifixion, since He was not crucified when the world was created. As Paul wrote, those who were saved were foreordained to salvation before Creation (cf. Ephesian 1:4).

Some hold that the book of life originally contained the names of every living person to be born in the world and that the names of the unsaved get blotted out when they die. This interpretation stems from Revelation 3:5, where Christ promised the believers in Sardis that their names would not be erased from the book of life, and from 22:19, where a person who rejects the messages in the book of Revelation is warned that "God will take away from him his share in the tree of life" (cf. "tree of life" in 2:7 and 22:2, 14 and "book of life" in 3:5; 17:8; 20:12, 15; 21:27). However, 13:8 probably means simply that those who are saved had their names written in the book of life in eternity past in anticipation of the death of Christ on the cross for them and that they will never be erased.

Taken together, verse 7 and 8 indicate the universal extent of the beast's political government as well as the final form of satanic religion in the Great Tribulation. Only those who come to Christ will be delivered from the condemnation that is involved.

The Exhortation to Hear

13:9–10. In a format similar to the exhortation to the seven churches of Asia Minor (chaps. 2–3), this passage gave an invitation to individuals who would listen. The dream of many today, of a universal church and a universal religion, will be realized in the end time, but it will be satanic and blasphemous instead of involving worship of the true God. In such a situation, appeal can only be made to individuals who will turn from it to God. In every age God speaks to those who will hear, a concept mentioned frequently in the Gospels (Matt. 11:15; 13:9, 43; Mark 4:9, 23; Luke 8:8; 14:35).

In contrast with the invitation addressed to the seven churches where each exhortation was addressed "to the church," the mention of churches is notably absent here. This is another indication that the church has been raptured before the time of these events.

Again, America, please view the movies *Apocalypse* by Jack Van Impee and *Left Behind* taken from the novel by Tim LaHaye and Jerry B. Jenkins to get a true idea of what our nation and the world is going to go through during the time the Lord Jesus Christ raptures His church, the Bride of Christ from the earth.

"Revelation, instead of being interpreted as addressed only to first-generation Christians facing persecution, is better understood as an exhortation to believers in all generation but especially those who will be living in the end time. Those who are willing to listen are reminded that their obedience to the Word of God may result in their captivity or martyrdom."

This is why it is very important that you give your heart to Christ by asking Him to forgive you of your sin and asking Him to come into your heart and life. You do not want to be in this earth after He raptures the church and see this world go through the Great Tribulation. You should also go to church each week but especially give your heart to the Lord Jesus Christ. I believe that He is going to help you because I pray for you constantly. I also believe that you should ask Him to help you. Also consider all things stated in chapter 16–18.

The exhortation closes. This calls for patient endurance (hypomonē, "steadfastness, perseverance" cf. 14:12) and faithfulness on the part of the saints; the ones who are "left behind" and become converted to Christianity.

Introduction of the Beast out of the earth

13:11–12. In contrast with the first beast who came "out of the sea" (v.1), the second beast came out of the earth. He was similar to the first beast (thērion, "a beast," was used of both personages). However, while the first beast was a Gentile, since he came from the entire human race as symbolized by "the sea" (v 1), the second beast was a creature of the earth. Some have taken this as a specific reference to the promised Land and have argued that he was therefore a Jew. There is no support of this in the context as the word for *earth* is the general word referring to the entire world (gē). Actually, his nationality and geographic origin are not indicated, and he is apparently the one referred to as "the false prophet" in 19:20 and 20:10. (For a comprehensive discussion of the two beasts, see Alford, *The Greek New Testament*, 4:678–79).

The second beast had two horns like a lamb, but he spoke like a dragon—that is, like Satan. From this it can be gathered that he was a religious character whose role was to support the political ruler, the first beast. He had great authority apparently derived from Satan and the political ruler, and he made the earth and its inhabitants worship the first beast, the one whose fatal wound had been healed.

Again, this tribulation period will be a very trying time. The Antichrist will be wounded in the head fatally, and Satan will raise him from the dead. There will be no hope for anyone on earth, but Christian people, which means you, will not take the mark of beast, 666, which means you can neither buy nor sell, which means you will have no food.

The false religious system, which was supported in this way, imitated the divine Trinity. Satan seeks to take the place of God the Father; the first beast assumes the place of Jesus Christ, the Son, the

King of Kings; and the second beast, the false prophet, has a role similar to the Holy Spirit who causes Christians to worship God. This is Satan's final attempt to substitute a false religion for true faith in Christ.

The Miracles of the Beast

13:13–15. To induce people to worship the first beast, the second beast performs great and miraculous signs (lit., "great signs," sémeia megala; cf. "a great . . . sign in 12:1), including fire from heaven. People sometimes overlook the fact that, while God can do supernatural things, Satan within certain limitations can also perform miracles, and he used this power in the fullest in this situation to induce people to worship Satan's substitute for Christ. Accordingly, the second beast deceived the inhabitant of the earth.

In addition to causing fire to come down from heaven, the second beast set up an image of the first beast.

The image was probably set up in the first temple in Jerusalem, which was taken over from the Jews. According to Paul (2 Thess. 2:4), the first beast actually sat in God's Temple at times and received worship, which properly belonged to God. Perhaps the beast's image was placed in the same temple to provide an object of worship when the beast himself was not there.

This image was mentioned frequently (Rev. 13:14–15; 14:9, 11; 15:2; 16:2; 19:20; 20:4). Whether the image was in the form of the world ruler, the first beast, or merely some object of worship is not clear, but it did seem to symbolize the power of the first beast.

The fact that the second beast could give breath to the image of the first beast, even making it speak, has created problems for expositors, for the Bible does not seem to indicate that Satan has the power to give life to an inanimate object. Only God is the Creator. So probably the beast's image is able to give an impression of breathing and speaking mechanically, like computerized talking robots today. There might be a combination of natural and supernatural powers to enable the beast out of the earth to accomplish his purpose. It apparently was quite convincing to people and induced them to worship the image (this is a theory only).

The command to worship the image as well as the first beast was enforced by killing those who refused to do so. But there was a difference between the decree to put them to death and its execution. The problem of ferreting out everyone in the entire earth who would not worship the beast would naturally that time. Hitler, in his attempt to exterminate the Jews, took many months and never completed his task. The multitude of martyrs is referred to in Revelation 7:9–17.

The Mark of the Beast

13:16–18. Enforcing his control over the human race and encouraging worship of the beast out of the sea, the second beast required everyone to receive a mark on his right hand or on his forehead (NIV) (KJV says in his right hand or in his forehead), and without this evidence that he had worshipped the beast, no one could buy or sell. The need to buy or sell such necessities as food and clothing would force each person in the entire world to decide whether to worship the beast or to bear the penalty. Apparently, the great majority worshipped the beast.

There has been much speculation on the insignia or mark of the beast, but it could be any of several kinds of identification. Countless attempts have been made to interpret the number 666, usually using the numerical equivalents of letters in the Hebrew, Greek, or other alphabets. As there probably have been hundreds of explanations continuing down to the present day, it is obvious that if the number refers to an individual, it is not clear to whom it refers. Again, please contact Word of Prophecy Ministries and Joan Veon through Southwest Radio Church or directly to obtain more information regarding this one world order.

Vaughn Shatzer in his video entitled *The New World Disorder*, says the mark of the beast (666) will be a microchip placed under the skin. We know that Texas Instruments has manufactured such a device already.

"Probably the best interpretation is that the number 6 would indicate that for all their pretentions to deity, Satan and the two beasts were just creatures and not the creator. That 6 is man's number is illustrated in the Bible, including the fact that man should work six days and rest the seventh. (For further discussion of the many views cf. Mounce, *The Book of Revelation*, pp. 263–65; Smith, *A Revelation of Jesus Christ*, pp. 206–7; and Walvoord, *Revelation*, pp. 209–12.)

The practice of gematria, the attempt to find hidden meanings in numbers in scripture, was prominent in the ancient world. Maybe John had in mind a particular person whom his close associates would be able to identify. Literature from the early church fathers, however, reveals the same confusion and variety of meanings that exist today, so probably it is best to leave this puzzle unsolved. Probably the safest conclusion is that of Thomas F. Torrance: "This evil trinity 666 apes the Holy Trinity 777, but always falls short and fails."

Chapter 13 is important because it introduces two of the main characters of Revelation: the beast out of the sea, the world dictator; and the beast out of the earth, the false prophet and chief supporter of the political ruler.

"Revelation 13, however, gives much insight into the character of the Great Tribulation." Again, "it will be a time of one world government and one world religion, with one world economic system" and a one world military. "Those who will resist the ruler and refuse to worship him will be subject to execution, and the martyrs may outnumber the believers who survive."

Please view the videos that continue from the movie *Apocalypse* such as *Tribulation and Revelation* by Jack Van Impee regarding what our nation, Israel, and the rest of the world will encounter concerning what people will suffer because of their faith in Jesus Christ. "It will be Satan's final and ultimate attempt to cause the world to worship him and to turn them from the worship of the true God and Jesus Christ as their Savior."

This chapter also makes it clear that the postmillennial dream of a world getting better and better through Christian effort and Gospel preaching is not supported in the Bible. Instead, the final form of world religion will be apostate, satanic, and blasphemous. These are many indications today that the world is heading in this direction, with the corresponding conclusion that the coming of the Lord is near.

In closing, I cannot stress the importance of you, America, knowing the truth of these end-time events. I write these words in fear and trembling. Afraid for the people that will be left behind, after the Rapture of the church and will have to suffer the seven-year tribulation period, especially the last three and a half years.

Please hear the words of the Lord Jesus Christ regarding the last days.

In Matthew 24:32–36, verse 36 says, "But of day and hour knoweth no man, no, not the angels of heaven, but my Father only." Verse 32–35 states, "Now learn a parable of the fig tree. When his branch is yet tender, and putteth forth leaves, ye know that summer is nigh.

> 33 So likewise ye, when ye shall see all these thing,
>   know that it is near even at the doors.

34 Verily I say unto you, This generation shall not pass till all these things be fulfilled.

35. Heaven and earth shall pass away, but my words shall not pass away."

America, that fig tree is the nation of Israel. She was rebirthed in 1948 (the month of May) after being destroyed over nineteen hundred years (in AD 70), and she has lain dormant all of that time, and now our generation is the generation that witnessed her rebirth. Jesus said this generation will see all these things: the "Rapture" of the church, that will usher in the seven-year tribulation period that is prompted by the Rapture.

Again, you do not want to be in this earth after the Rapture takes place. But if you are left behind and have to suffer the tribulation, the last three and a half years will be much more severe, but you can survive it. Only do not take the mark of the beast, which is the number 666.

Lastly, America, God is not a liar. We can trust His Word. He said in Matthew 24:35, "Heaven and earth shall pass away, but my word shall not pass away." Trust God's Word. To trust His Word is trust Him. Let Him into your heart, ask Him to forgive you of sin, and invite the Lord Jesus Christ to be the Lord of your life.

Thank you, Reverend Hutchings and Southwest Radio Church for being there for me and others during the eighties, nineties, even until now.

Yours in Christ,
Alvin R. Ervin

An Apology to Walmart

July 22, 2020

From: Alvin R. Ervin, Preacher of the Gospel

To: Facebook Family/Entire Body of Christ
    Walmart Department Stores
    All U.S. Police Departments
    Texas Governor, Abbot
    President, Donald Trump

Dear Facebook Family,

Please join me as I prayerfully apologize to ALL Walmart Department Stores for purposely not wearing a face covering, setting a standard for Texans and all Citizens of the US. Trusting God according to His promise to rescue us from every trap and protect us from the fatal plague (diseases; Coronavirus). His Word says do not be afraid of the terrors of the night, nor fear the dangers of the day. Nor dread the pestilence that stalks in darkness... (Psalm 91:3, 5-6)

The weekend of July 17, 2020 I was escorted from location FM 3040 Walmart Store by Walmart Security. There were bitter, sweet moments while walking beside the security officer as he escorted me to the exit door. The reason not wearing a mask somewhat took me by surprise. A few weeks before the COVID19 escalated. Governor Abbot announced all Texans are encouraged (or required) to wear a face covering. I had been approached by an employee at the FM 407 location in Highland Village, a nice little town (maybe upper crust, lake front homes of Lake Lewisville) near North Lewisville, Tx where I live.

When approached at the 407 location a women entered the store shorty after me. She spoke with the gentleman that had approached me and turned around and exited the store.

I had been allowed to enter both stores because I frequent them quite often. There is a Walmart location on Main St. in Lewisville I frequent even more. Again many people know me. There is a White lady that attends the same Church I tended in Flower Mound, near Lewisville, another small city of which I formerly lived (definitely upper crust).

When escorted from the FM 3040 location the bitter moments were; I have never had problems with City Officials or the law because of the way that I a raised by my grandmother Celester Dotsey and mother Eddie L. Jordan. 12 grades of public school never called to the principals office for misconduct, was trained by grandmother until 12 years of age to attend Church every Sunday, to never caused problems in our community, or any other place. I moved to Temple, Tx at age 12 living with my mother, trained to stay home and only visit and socialize with close friends like Grady and Jackie whom I grew up with. Because of my home training while employed at Texas Instruments (TI) near 19 years, never had issues on the job that caused reprimanding for work ethic or any other reason but was scrutinize.

My tenure at TI began in the late 60's after the death of Dr. Martin Luther King. I purposely kept my nose clean because I liked my reputation, and still a little fond of it today. The Apostle Peter in I Peter 3:16 states "give no man, no reason to speak ill (evil) of you." I was taught those words by my grandmother and it worked well for me.

I trained my son Terrence in the same manner that I way trained. We attended Church together. He was 9 years old when we both gave our lives to to the Lord Jesus Christ. When he was accused of doing things he did not do, I wrote a letter to the judge and attorney involved, that letter is now available to the public.

Being scrutinized on the job at TI was something that I was made aware of by observance. Knowing that I was working among many Whites that may not like a Black man that had become somewhat popular on the job, I had to keep my nose clean while also enjoying life.

A White friend, Roger, and I had great Company Parties. We kept a large crowd following. During those days I loved to dance. Roger could spin a record as well as any professional disc jockey. Many people joined us. Whether at the club house of the apartments where I lived or at a discotheque (disco) where we frequent, like the Koo Koos Nest above the famous Don Carter's bowling lanes in Dallas near North Park. White lady friends of Roger liked me also. They especially like dancing with me, one in particular. Again, I knew that I was being scrutinized so I had to be careful. This little lady did like me; we dated briefly as well as a couple of Hispanics. But we were never called to the principal's office (smile). Our parties were very clean (no drugs nor brawls or such). The president of the company attended our party at the Koo Koos Nest and had a nice time, even danced a couple of times, which honored Roger and I. During that era Texas Instruments was the second larges electronic company in the U. S. (some say on the planet).

Roger was acquainted with Don Carter who had his own TV Program as well as the bowling lanes, a world champion bowler. Roger had bowled a perfect score in a tournament at Carter's Bowling Lanes and received a ring for excellence, he was highly visible on the job as well. His dad was a upper level manager at TI. But most follow me because they consider him a snob (I was told). He always treated me really well. And he was a few younger, may he honor me and knew I did not play around irresponsibly.

The sweet moments of the escort form Walmart were obvious. All efforts we put forth to honor God are to glorify Christ among others. In the book of Acts, Peter and John were commanded not to teach or preach in the Name of Jesus. Peter stated "We ought to obey God rather than men. ...When they called the Apostles, and beaten them, they commanded that they should not speak in the name of Jesus, and let they go. And they *(the apostles)* departed from the presence of the council, <u>rejoicing</u> that they were <u>counted worthy</u> to suffer shame *(the shame of beating)* for his *(Jesus)* name. (Acts 5:12-41 KJV).

What we do to honor God by Glorifying Christ will be spoken of in heaven through out eternity. God's Word says the apostles rejoiced that they were counted worthy to suffer shame for his name. I did experience shame as the security officer escorted me to exit, but it was sweet to know that I suffered shame because I was counted worthy by God Almighty. He promised to rescue us from every trap and protect us from the fatal plague (diseases; Coronavirus). He said do not be afraid of the terrors of the night, nor fear the dangers of the day. Nor dread the pestilence (Coronavirus) that stalks in darkness... I did not use a face covering to cause problem but to set a standard for the American People (especially Texans). To ALL Walmart Stores FORGIVE ME, it may occur again.

The nation of Sweden has not had a lock down since the spread of the virus began. It's economy thrives as all nations, by the people continuing as normal. Sweden does not glorify God but it seems as if God is using Sweden to make us jealous as stated in His Word. We as Americans are suppose to be the most Godliest nation on the planet. We should set the standard for the world to see us trust God's promises. Dear God FORGIVE US!

To all police departments through the US, know that you are being prayed for, and all that we do to set a standard for the Americans people is not to create issues with the laws of the land but to encourage God's people in their faith.

Governor Abbot, we are praying for you. We've heard you honor God in the past, please do not stop now. We see the people of this nation honoring the requirements of the leaders, now would be a great time to lead in them in Godliness. We ask you and all governors to request their prayers and have to join me in returning prayer to all our schools, we need God's help. This nation was established by faith in God. He is the God of our Fathers. We owe to Him and them to return prayer to our schools.

Mr. President you would do really well in signing the most important executive order any president can ever sign by over turning the Supreme Court decision to remove prayer from our schools. You are prayed for daily regarding this matter and we pray He grant you that authority. Please honor God all of you leaders in this nation lest a worst thing comes upon us. He will not stop. His Word declares "Whom the Lord loves He chastises."

Facebook Family, thanks for joining me in this prayer, God Bless You.

To Governor Gregg Abbot
   President Donald Trump
   And The American People

August 10. 2020
Dear Facebook Family,

Please join me is praying for Gov. Gregg Abbot and President Trump in leading Texas and the American People in a more Godly manner that will encourage Americans to trust God through the pandemic ahead of us. The American people seem to be trusting our leaders unconditionally regarding the pestilence (called coronavirus COVID19) that is upon us.

God gave *(the Father of our Christian Faith and the Father of our Nation) Abram, (whom He would change his name to Abraham),* a promise and stated "I will make you a father of many nations." When God gave Abraham that promise, Abraham's wife Sarah could not bear a child, she was barren:

> Genesis 11:29-30 says "And Abram and Nahor took them wives: the name of Abram's was Sarai *(that God would change to Sarah)*; and the name of Nahor's wife, Milcah, the daughter of Haran, the father of Milcah, and the father of Iscah.
> 30 But Sarai was barren, she had no child.
> Genesis 12:1-4 says, "Now the Lord had said unto Abram, 'get thee out of thy country, and from thy kindred and from thy father's house, unto a land that I will shew thee.

2 And I will make of thee a great nation, and I will bless thee, and make thy name great and thou *(you)* shalt be a blessing:

3 And I will bless them that bless them that thee, and curse him that curseth thee: and in thee shall all families of the earth be blessed.

Because of God's promise to Israel in verse 3, this nation still supports God's chosen people. He said "I will bless the nations that bless you (Israel) and I will curse the nations that curse you.

4 So Abram departed, as the Lord had spoken unto him; and Lot went with him and Abram was seventy and five *(75)* years old when he departed out of Haran.

When God gave Abraham the promise "You will be a father of many nation, many years past. When God called Moses to lead the Children of Israel out of Egypt, the Lord began to refer to Himself to the People of Israel as "the God of your fathers, I am the God of fathers, the God of Abraham, Isaac, and Jacob." We know that Abraham begat Isaac, and Isaac begat Jacob whom God changed his name to Israel. Jacob/Israel begat twelve sons, all of whom became nations (or states), those twelve states became the nation of Israel, that stands today.

Fast forwarding to the United States; this nation was established by the Puritans. They of course were called Puritans because they were Christians of which means their hearts were Pure of which the term or name Puritans came forth. When we in this nation refer to God as the God of our Fathers, we are not speaking of our founding fathers (George Washington, Thomas Jefferson, John Adam; these men gained our declaration of independence, of which we honor every 4th July), they only carried what was already established by our fore Fathers, the Puritans whose hearts were Pure before God. Thus God in this nation will ever be referred to as the God of our Fathers, just as it stated in God <u>Holy Word.</u>

This Word is for all Muslims, Hindus, Budish, Native Americans and ALL worshipers of ALL other Gods in these United States, this is still a CHRISTIAN nation established by our fore Father and will ever be a Christian Nation. You are a guest in this house (called America), let us as Christians serve you. The Church, (Church Leaders) are not stepping up to declare to you the truth, because it is not political correct, just as they are following our leaders in wearing face covering dictated by secular (un-Godly leaders). We are to obey the laws of the land and also encourage God's people to trust Him. He (God) has brought this disease upon us because of our disobedience, turning our backs to the Him, the God of our Fathers. And He is now able to use this virus to chastise us in a greater way, because the Church is suppose to lead the way, turning the hearts of the people toward God, to worship and serve Him and ask Him to forgive us for removing Prayer out of our schools, to ask Him to forgive us of abortion and same sex marriages.

Homosexuals, God loves you as much as any person on this planet. John 3:16 states, "God so loved the world (every person on the planet), that He gave His only Son that whosoever believes in Him shall not perish but have eternal life. Christ died for the sin of all man kind, no matter what the sin, His Blood can wash away the sin. But it has to be confessed. 1st John 1:9 says "If we confess our sin, He *(God)* <u>is faithful and just to forgive us</u> <u>our sins, and to cleanse us from all unrighteousness.</u>

Homosexuality is a sin before God. It doesn't mean He loves you any less, it means He wants you to confess that filth. Please know that I am not judging you. He said we should not judge other, but speak the truth in Love. Again, His Word says "Judge not, that you be not judged. Homosexuality is worst kind of sin that can be confessed. His Word says it is an abomination before God. There are things in my life I have to confess daily as a weakness. It doesn't mean that I sin against Him in the weak areas everyday, I confess to Him daily because He is a Holy God and has a pure heart. Christ says "they that worship God should worship Him in Spirit and In Truth. Truth to me means a Pure Heart. In Psalms 24:4-5 David says, "He that hath clean hands, and a pure heart, who hath not lifted soul unto vanity, not sworn deceitfully.

5 He shall receive the blessings from the Lord and righteousness from the God of his salvation. (King James Version).

1st Chronicles 21:1 says, "Satan rose up against Israel and caused David to take a census of the Israelites. Ordering this census by David displeased God.

> 14 So the Lord sent pestilence (*a disease such as the coronavirus COVID19 or some other deadly virus*) upon Israel: and there fell of Israel seventy thousand men.

> 15 And God sent an angel unto Jerusalem to destroy it: and as he was destroying the Lord beheld, and he repented Him of the evil and said to the angel that destroyed, It is enough, stay no thine hand. And the angel of the Lord stood by the threshing floor of Ornan the Jebusite.

16And David lifted up his eyes, and saw the angel of the Lord stand <u>between the earth and the heaven, having a drawn sword in his hand stretched out over Jerusalem.</u> Then David and elders of Israel, who were clothed in sackcloth fell upon their faces.

17 And David said unto god, is it not I that commanded the people to be number? Even I it is that have sinned and done evil indeed; but as for these sheep what have they done? Let thine hand, I pray thee, O Lord my God be on me and on my father's house; but not on thy people, that they should be plagued.

18 Then the angel of the Lord commanded Gad to say to David that David should go up and set up an altar unto the Lord in the threshing floor of Ornan the Jebusite.

Nothing comes on this earth except God allows it; in some circumstances He orders it such as the disease spoken above in Chronicles. When God's people began to disobey Him, He said He would chastise them because of His love for them and do not want them to get any deeper in sin. Hebrews 12:1b ..." let us strip off every weight that slows us sown, especially the sin that so easily hinders our progress. And let us run with endurance the race that God has set before us.

2 We do this by keeping our eyes on Jesus, on <u>whom our faith depends from start to finish.</u> He was will to die a shameful death on the cross because of the joy He knew would be His afterward. Now he is seated in place of highest honor beside God's throne in heaven.

3 Think about all He endured when sinful people did such terrible things to Him, so that you don't become weary and give up.

4 After all, you have not yet given your lives in your struggle against.

5 And have you entirely forgotten the encouraging Words god spoke to you his children? He spoke to you, His children? He said:

'My child, don't ignore it when the Lord disciplines (*chastises*) you, and don't be discouraged when he corrects (*disciplines*) you.

For the Lord disciplines those he loves, and He punishes those he accepts as his children.

7 As you endure this divine discipline, remember that God is treating you as His own children. Who ever heard of a child who was never disciplined?

8 Since we respect our earthly fathers who disciplined us, should we not all the more cheerfully submit to the discipline of our Heaven Father and live forever?! (New Living Translation).

Governor Abbot, you and every governor in this nation should have informed your state this truth. Especially you Governor Abbot, because we in Texas have heard you speak of your faith in the past. You, Mr. President should have encouraged all Governors to speak these Word from God's Holy Bible Months ago. God's servant posted on ARE Outreach a 4 part message to this nation from Psalms 91 that should have gotten the attention of every person in the U. S. and others around the world; and no one acknowledged those sermons. Now God is helping me to reach out to you in a more stern manner before all the people of this nation and other nation as well.

The people of this nation is following the dictates of all Governors regarding this pandemic, and all governors should encourage every person in their state to attend church every Sunday and seek God, praying for His help. We need His help and as He delivers us, (and He will deliver us) we should never stop thanking Him for that deliverance. <u>He is worthy of all praise, thanks, glory, and honor, His Word declares. It says that we should Worship Him!!! and ask Him to FORGIVE US.</u>

Facebook book family, please pray with me, spread the Word, and encourage our leaders to do what God says.

God Bless You,
I Love You,

ARErvin